## Heart VIII

Made in 2009

30¼" x 41¾" (77cm x 106cm)

Hand appliqué, embroidery, machine piecing, cotton,
No. 5 embroidery thread

I thought I'd make this one with a slightly different palette than usual,
choosing some gentle colors. The hearts are few in number and set
on the blocks in a rough manner, placed freely so that they extend
past the blocks in places. I decided to cover the quilt in rough stitches
made with No. 5 embroidery thread, but once I began it seemed
as though no matter how I stitched I could never fill it all up! I wish
I had included more of these rough lines, but it was not to be...

ISBN 978-1-57421-425-3

Goke Keiko no Quilt Zukuri
Copyright © 2009 by Keiko Goke and NIHON VOGUE-SHA. All rights reserved.
English translation © 2012 Design Originals, an imprint of Fox Chapel Publishing Company.
Photographer: Akinori Miyashita (with interview photography by Kana Watanabe)
Illustrations: Michiko Watanuki
Planning editor: Toshie Yano
Editing assistants: Sakae Suzuki and Noriko Hachimonji
Book design: Washizu Design Office
Translator: Claire Tanaka
First published in Japan in 2009 by Nihon Vogue Co., Ltd., Tokyo
English language translation rights arranged with Nihon Vogue Co., Ltd., Tokyo, through Japan Foreign-Rights Centre

*All My Thanks and Love to Quilting* is an unabridged translation of the original Japanese book. This version published
by Design Originals, 1970 Broad St., East Petersburg, PA 17520.

Library of Congress Cataloging-in-Publication Data
Goke, Keiko.
 [Goke keiko no kirutozukuri. English]
 All my thanks and love to quilts : art quilts created by Keiko Goke / Keiko Goke. -- First [edition].
    pages cm
 Summary: "Keiko Goke is a world renowned quilter and fabric designer. This book chronicles 70 original quilts. There are eight
themes of collections such as traditional, applique, alphabet, heart, circle, log cabin, Japanese fabric and the author's favorite.
There also are step-by-step instructions for design and piecing with illustrations and photos"-- Provided by publisher.
 ISBN 978-1-57421-425-3 (pbk.)
 1. Goke, Keiko--Themes, motives. 2. Quilting--Patterns. I. Title.
 TT835.G6213 2012
 746.46--dc23
               2012011587

Printed in China
First Printing

# *All My Thanks and Love to* QUILTS

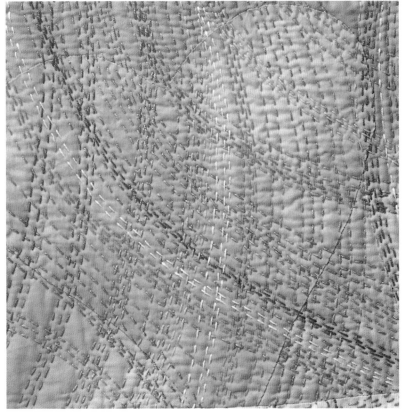

ART QUILTS CREATED BY KEIKO GOKE

Design Originals

an Imprint of Fox Chapel Publishing

www.d-originals.com

# To Begin

## Flower Shop Kei

Made in 1986
39½" x 35" (100cm x 89cm)

Handmade applique, quilting, embroidery, cotton

Once upon a time, I was obsessed with flower shops. I remembered this about myself and made my own *Flower Shop Kei*. I've never studied embroidery techniques, but I feel nostalgic now when I remember how absorbed I became in embroidering the flowers for this piece.

Forty years! Oh, these forty years have passed so fast. If I hadn't one day found a piece on patchwork in a magazine at my design company and started quilting, I imagine I'd be a different person today.

Surely!

The quilts I was making by myself and for myself changed me in a big way. First, people practically forced me to start teaching a class, though I had no qualifications and I didn't know what or how to teach it, and I'd never learned anything anywhere…

I'm so grateful to those people who came to the class!

If I'd only been making quilts on my own, I don't think I would have been able to continue working at quilting in such a serious fashion. At that time I was terribly shy, so it took a while before someone told me that during that period, I'd been "scary."

Thirty years have passed since I started those lessons in my home. The quilts I made with everyone together, I entered into so many contests. And thanks to that, I was able to make friends overseas, and I had many opportunities to work abroad. My roots haven't changed, but quilts changed even my personality. I'm so grateful to quilts for broadening my world in many ways!

And then, and then, best of all I'm happy that I'm able to bring these past forty years together in such a way. I'm grateful from the bottom of my heart for this opportunity to show off everything from my first fumbling steps, to my most recent works.

—Keiko Goke

Who ran back to Sendai as soon as she graduated from Setsu Mode Seminar? Me. I was only in Tokyo for two years, but I felt, "I just can't live in Tokyo!" Who put her designs in a big bag and walked around to all the design companies? Me. And who, when she was told by a big firm, "You can come work with us," decided to work at a little place instead? Me.

I guess I'm a bit of a contrarian?

But that place shut down almost immediately. The next design company I worked for had a pile of magazines for reference, which is where I first encountered quilting, in the form of a simple cushion made of connecting squares.

# Contents

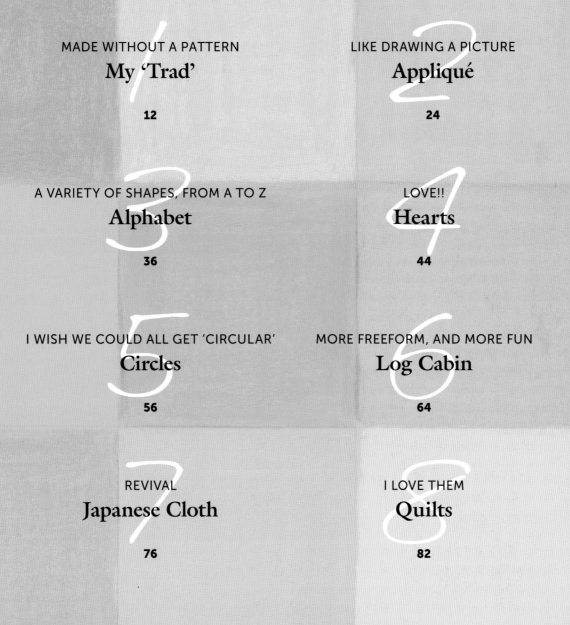

Quilts that emerge from daily life in my studio **4**

Keiko Goke's Quiltmaking (From Heart VIII) **6**

MADE WITHOUT A PATTERN
## *1* My 'Trad'
**12**

LIKE DRAWING A PICTURE
## *2* Appliqué
**24**

A VARIETY OF SHAPES, FROM A TO Z
## *3* Alphabet
**36**

LOVE!!
## *4* Hearts
**44**

I WISH WE COULD ALL GET 'CIRCULAR'
## *5* Circles
**56**

MORE FREEFORM, AND MORE FUN
## *6* Log Cabin
**64**

REVIVAL
## *7* Japanese Cloth
**76**

I LOVE THEM
## *8* Quilts
**82**

PATTERNS AND INSTRUCTIONS
## How to Make the Quilts
**97**

# Quilts that emerge from daily life in my studio...

Almost all year-round I'm in this room—for work, for rest, and even to sleep.

When I moved in, it was a much bigger space, but over time it's begun to overflow with all kinds of stuff.

To tell the truth, it won't all fit in this room, and the clutter has spread to the next room. I keep thinking I've got to do something about it...

When I look around, there are mountains of things that have nothing to do with quilts!

There are some cheap antiques I used to love hunting around for, and some pottery I made long ago. Then, there are the wooden *kokeshi* dolls I've started collecting recently, and among them are several of the "izumekko" variety that I particularly like. Oh, and I love baskets, so there are lots of those, too.

But all these things that have nothing to do with work is why I love this room so much! Well, I think that must be the reason, anyway.

Of course fabric is very important to me, but other things are special, too.

# Keiko Goke's Quiltmaking
## —From Heart VIII—

I've got a lot of fabric in my house. So much that I sometimes think I'll never be able to use it all up. One reason I've been able to have such a long relationship with quilting was that class I started, and another is that quilting became a form of self-expression for me. I've never studied quilting. I'm self-taught. Perhaps because I never regarded anything in quilting as off-limits, it felt the same as painting a picture.

To draw a picture, you need paints. WIth paints, you can mix the colors together to get the shade you like, but fabric doesn't work that way. Even with a single red, you might find you need a slightly different shade of red. That's why, if I go somewhere and I find some fabric I like, I can't help but snap it up, and the result is my mountain of fabric. I imagine all quilters have similar fabric mountains of their own. With fabric as my paint, I've had a long relationship with quilting. I wonder how long I will continue on this wonderful quilting journey…

My beloved hearts are even on the mug I like to use!

While making some rough sketches, I decide on a simple heart design.

When I start adding color to my favorite rough sketch, that's when it gets fun...

Next, I pull out cloth I think I will be able to use to make the *Heart VIII* I've got in my head. The most fun by far is choosing the colors! Once I do it, I feel as though I'm halfway done.

## 1 Selecting a Quilt Design

When I was trying to decide which quilt to use for the cover, naturally the first thing that spring to mind was the hearts! Lately, my colors have been changing little by little. I decided to make the hearts slightly different colors than what I have used up to now. And I thought I'd like to cover the whole thing in large, rough stitches like I haven't done for some time.

**Before anything is finalized, I pull out all the colors I've got in mind, plus a few extra.**

When I begin choosing from this selection, I found it hard to shun the colors that were close to my usual vibrant hearts...

Softer colors can create a slightly different impression, too...

**The first stage in selecting colors.**

## 2 Make a life-size pattern and select the fabric.

I often make quilts without a pattern, but having a pattern sometimes helps the process go faster. This time I made a pattern. It's relatively easy to make a little rough sketch, but hard to convert it to actual size. Enlarging the little sketch on a copy machine is one way to do it, but I don't mind if it is only somewhat like the original drawing, so I draw the life-size pattern myself.

I prepare a large piece of paper and draw while referring to my sketch. I keep the overall balance of space in mind while I draw.

I draw my life-size pattern, then try placing the fabric colors I've chosen on it.

Once I've placed fabric on the entire design, I take another look at the overall color balance and set my color choices.

At this point, all the colors have been selected.

## 3 Cut the fabric and appliqué it.

When appliquéing the hearts, there's no need to start from the edge. It's perfectly all right to start anywhere, so start sewing from the block where you feel "this color has to go here!" Once you've got one done, it's easier to see what color should go beside it, so I think it gets easier to select the colors.

I lay the pattern on the back side of the background fabric and mark it with a water-soluble pen or pencil. I make a ⅜" (1cm) seam allowance and cut the fabric.

In the same way, I cut out the heart part of the pattern and then lay it on the material and mark it. With the heart, mark the front side of the fabric.

For the heart, I make a ¼" (7mm) seam allowance and cut the fabric.

Baste just the heart, and pin it down on the background fabric to do the appliqué.

Sew the parts of the heart where it dips and points carefully with a slip stitch.

After you finish appliquéing, cut out the background fabric from the back side of the heart.

Follow the same procedure for the other eleven blocks. Then, slip stitch all twelve of them together. The quilt top is finished!

The heart shapes you cut out from the background fabric can be used on another project someday.

## 4  Baste, then stitch.

I think the most enjoyable part of making a quilt is the quilting itself. I enjoy quilting by hand, quilting with a machine, and sewing chunky stitches with thick thread like I did this time. In any case, through quilting, what was once just a quilt top becomes so much more expressive, and that's just unbearably lovely.

Do some stitches in place of the quilting. First, layer the quilt top with batting and a backing, and baste the whole thing. Pin basting is also an option.

Once the basting is done, start stitching with No. 5 embroidery thread.

Marks made with a pencil won't come off, so use a hera marker or something similar to mark the base stitch lines with temporary creases, and sew along those lines.

At first you'll sew and sew and it feels like it'll you'll never be finished, but then you'll start to enjoy it and it'll be hard to stop!

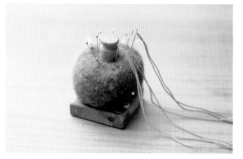

It makes it easier if you thread several colors you think you'll use and keep them at the ready.

It's fun if you can make the stitches with as many different colors of No. 5 thread as possible.

## 5 Do the binding and the quilt's done!

Binding is the finishing touch. It can really change the look of a quilt. Even just one aspect of the binding, such as the color or width, can make a difference, so lay down lots of different colors of fabric before choosing one. In one method, the binding fabric doesn't show on the front. If I don't want to have another color around the edges of my work, I often use this method to finish a quilt.

Once I'm finished stitching, I cut the outside edges straight.

This time, I choose a fabric that has different colors all over it.

I use my sewing machine to sew the 1⅝" (4cm)-wide fabric around the four sides of the quilt.

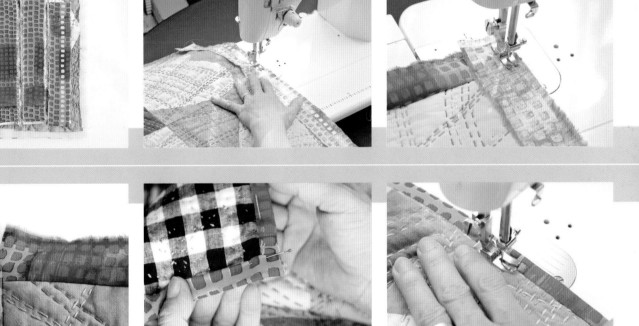

Fold it over to the finished width, baste it, and machine stitch along the front. Do a careful topstitch close to the edge of the bunting.

All done!

# My 'Trad'

When I first encountered quilts, I made the same kind of traditionally ("trad") patterned quilts that everyone else did. But at some point, I realized that even if I changed the fabric, all my quilts looked like something I'd seen before, and I began to think, "I want to make something a little different, different than other people's!" I've been making original quilts ever since. But in the past few years, for some reason I've begun to find myself attracted to trad patterns, and when I look at them, I just don't think I would be able to make one the prim and proper way. I wondered if I could make one without a paper pattern. I looked for a design like that and gave trad another try!

Right now, I've made five patterns, and it's lots of fun! I'd like to try making some other patterns one day.

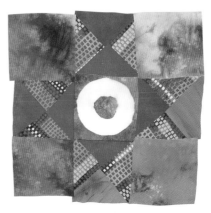

Here, I've decide to try my hand at an Ohio Star. All the patterns are the same, but I selected the fabric for each piece of this block, cut it, and line deverything up. The cuts don't need to be exact: try being bold!

Once I've decided the colors for all the pieces and I'm finished cutting, I start sewing it together from whatever part feels right. In the case of this pattern, I made each square first, then assembled each set of nine, then I sewed it all together. I think it's amusing and fun how neither the angles on the triangles nor the squares match up exactly.

**My Ohio Star**

Made in 1996

63" x 60" (157cm x 152cm)

Machine piecing, quilting, hand embroidery, cotton

This work is something I made much earlier than my other trad without pattern pieces. I used a lot of Debra Lunn's hand-dyed fabric, which I encountered when I was taking a lot of trips to the United States.

Debra Lunn was the first artist to create hand-dyed gradation fabric for quilting in the United States in the 1970s. She has won many awards for her quilts, including the prestigious Quilt National. She dyes her own fabrics in order to create the exact colors she needs for her creative quilts.

**Rob Peter to Pay Paul A**

Made in 2008

70" x 70" (180cm x 180cm)

Machine piecing, quilting, cotton

Recently, I've rediscovered my interest in trad patterns. This quilt is the first one I made when I decided I'd try to see how far I could go in making trad patterns without a paper pattern. I'd always thought this would be a fun one to try making without a pattern. I decided to start by sewing the small blocks in the center. I wasn't really thinking about the final outcome. Once it reached a certain size, I started thinking about what to do next. I eventually decided to surround the center with some blocks that were double the size of the center ones. Once I finished piecing, I surrounded the outside edges with a bunch of stripes of fabric that I'd sewn together, and the result was a quilt I like very much.

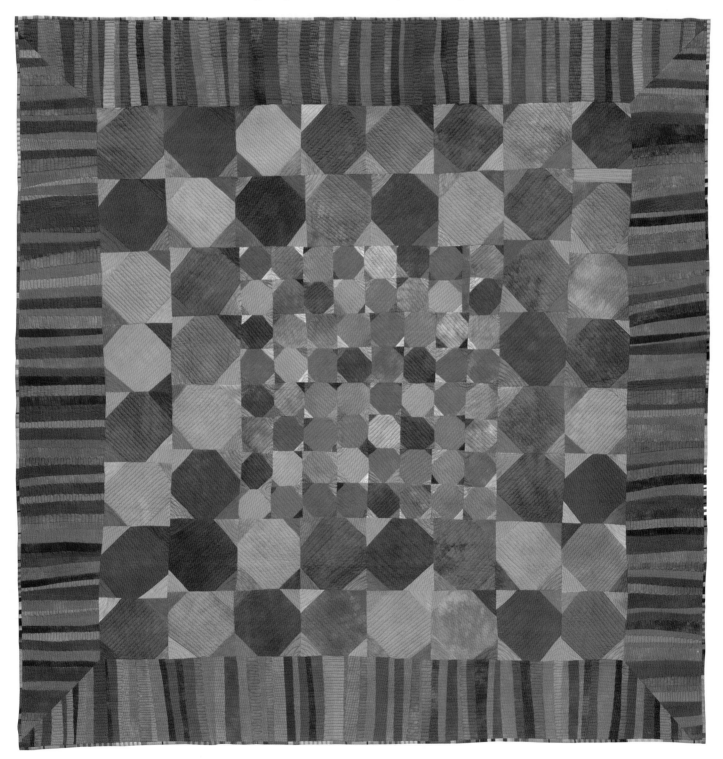

## Rob Peter to Pay Paul B

Made in 2008

27½" x 28½" (70cm x 72cm)

Machine piecing, quilting, cotton

I had a lot of scraps of fabric left from when I made *Rob Peter to Pay Paul A*. This is the quilt I made with them. First, I took the triangular scraps and sewed them together to make squares, and then I combined them all.

## Rob Peter to Pay Paul C

Made in 2008

19½" x 22" (50cm x 56cm)

Machine piecing, quilting, hand embroidery, cotton

After I used my scraps to make *Rob Peter to Pay Paul B*, I used those scraps to make one more little tapestry.

# Making a Rob Peter to Pay Paul Quilt without a Pattern

First, prepare 4¾" (12cm) squares of the fabric you plan to use for the center of your piece, and put them on your cutting mat. Cut four or five pieces at a time (make nine squares).

Prepare some roughly cut triangles. I used 36.

The square is in the middle with four triangles on top. Keep the colors in mind while laying out the pattern.

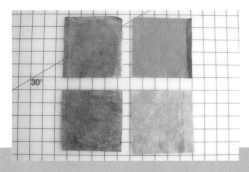

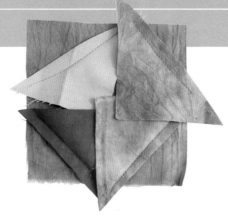

Once you're happy with it, sew the a triangle onto each of the four corners of the square.

Use a rotary cutter to trim the extra fabric. Make nine blocks.

Lay out the nine blocks and decide the placement.

Sew the nine blocks together.

Iron the seam allowances.

Flatten out the seam allowances like this.

The overall impression can change depending on how the blocks are arranged.

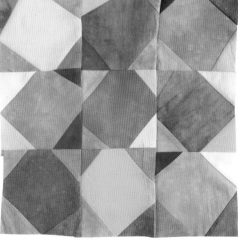

Sew it together and it's done.

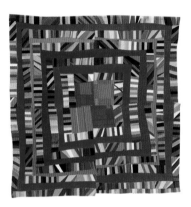

## My Log Cabin

Made in 2008

74 ½" x 74 ½" (190cm x 190cm)

Machine piecing, quilting, cotton

This is one of my trad without a pattern quilts. I made four quarters of a log cabin, and sewed them together. The striped part is made of 8" (20cm) squares of striped fabric that I randomly sewed together and then cut in half to use here.

## My House

Made in 2008

78" x 78" (198cm x 198cm)

Machine piecing, quilting, cotton

Another of my trad without a pattern quilts. I really wanted to try the house pattern, so here it is! I found a pattern I thought I could do inside a collection of trad patterns, and I made a quilt using some colors that are a little different than my usual. For the lattice, I used striped fabric to create some movement among the houses, which can tend to be quite staid.

## My Basket

Made in 2008

88" x 76" (224cm x 193cm)

Machine piecing, quilting, hand appliqué, cotton

To make the large triangular part of the baskets, I stacked four squares of fabric, cut them, rearranged the colors, sewed them into blocks, and then cut them in half. Use a rotary cutter and cut the basket handles freehand.

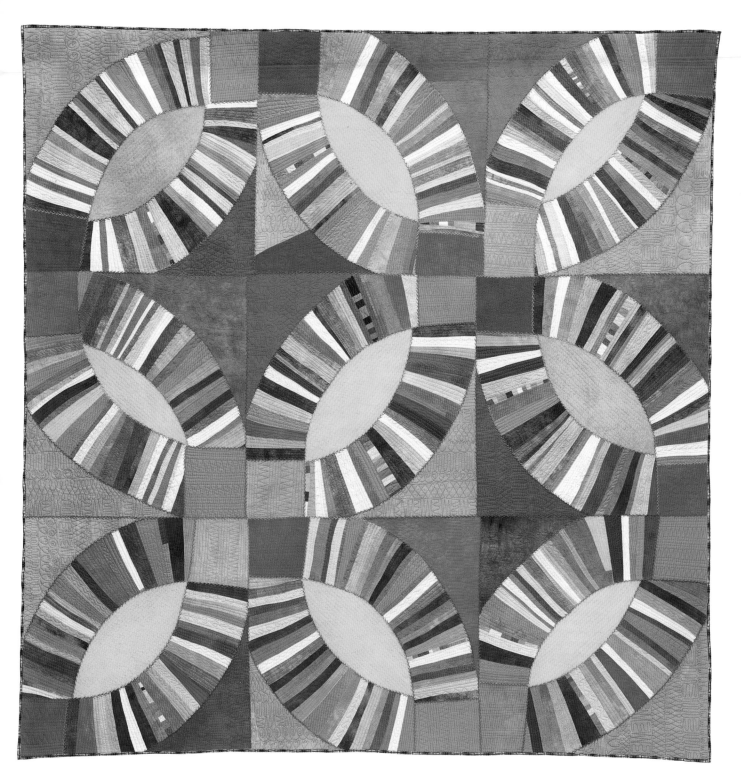

Made in 2008

88" x 86 ½" (224cm x 220cm)

Machine piecing, quilting, hand embroidery

**My Double Wedding Ring**

This was my second trad without a pattern quilt. At first, I was worried about whether I'd be able to do it or not, but I somehow succeeded in making a double wedding ring. In all, it has nine blocks. I love how none of them match up exactly! I was delighted when I finished it.

# Making a Basket Quilt without a Pattern

Stack four different colors of 7⅞" (20cm)-square fabric and cut three lines through them.

Rearrange the colors and make four new squares.

Sew the rearranged squares together.

Cut the squares in half diagonally. Each of these will become the large triangles used for the baskets.

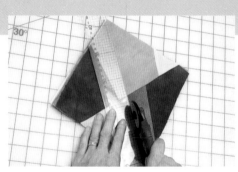

Choose and cut fabric for the bottom two smaller triangles, the side parts, and the top. Appliqué a handle onto the top part.

Sew the two smaller triangles on the bottom to the side parts, then sew them to the large triangle. Sew the top half with the handle appliquéd on to the bottom half, and a single basket block is complete.

Cut the excess fabric from the completed blocks.

# Making a Double Wedding Ring Quilt without a Pattern

Make striped fabric by piecing together strips of pretty fabric. Make a stock of striped fabric when the mood strikes; it's handy to have to use when needed.

Cut the striped fabric into 7⅞" (20cm) widths. Then, cut it in several places, and insert trapezoidal segments here and there to create a smooth curve...

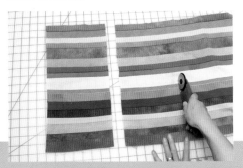

Once it has a smooth curve, sew it together. If it isn't curved enough, cut it somewhere and insert another trapezoidal segment.

Cut the blue pieces for the middle and outside to match the lines of the double wedding ring. Place it all together, and if it fits, sew it.

Sew the blue fabric on the inside and outside edges, and iron.

Cut away any excess fabric once everything is sewn together.

Cut all the parts and arrange them together.

One completed block.

# Appliqué

Made in 2004

50" x 50" (127cm x 127cm)

### A Present For You

Machine piecing, quilting, hand appliqué, embroidery, cotton

In my case, designs always come to me sudddenly. Like, "A giant gift box!!" I made this quilt based on an actual-sized design I drew.

I love beach glass and I went to the seaside year after year, picking it up and collecting it. I've got mountains of it in my house. I've given a lot away, but there's still plenty left.

When I'd just started making quilts, I really only made traditionally patterned quilts. I started making appliquéd quilts as a way to make something different than other people. I thought, "If I draw a picture, and make it into an appliqué, then maybe I'll be able to make my own original work." About 1980 I really got into making appliqué works. Appliqué is fun in a different way than piecing. Why not try drawing your own picture and making an applique quilt?

### All My Favorite Things!

Made in 1987

37½" x 31½" (95cm x 80cm)

Hand appliqué, embroidery, cotton

I like flowers, and balloons, and rainbows, and marbles... This is a random collection of my favorite things. I made the appliquéd parts by drawing a life-size paper pattern, and embroidered things freehand as I thought of them.

### We're Home!

Made in 1980

60½" x 40" (154cm x 102cm)

Hand piecing, appliqué, embroidery, cotton

I made several picture quilts with children as the theme when my own two children were small. This quilt is one of those, made at a time when I was very busy raising my children. It shows me coming home after a day out shopping with the children. To our family waiting at home, we say, "We're home!"

## Worrying Cactus

Made in 2003

67" x 70" (170cm x 176cm)

Hand appliqué, embroidery, machine quilting, cotton, No. 5 embroidery thread, No. 30 rainbow thread

This is the third work in my *Cactus* series. I worried a lot over this design, which I named *Worrying Cactus*. I trekked to gardening shops and searched for many designs. When I finally found a cactus shaped like this, I thought, "Yay!"

# Use the Fusing Method to Make Cactus Spots

This time, choose six colors of fabric. Put double-sided fusible interfacing on a safe surface and prepare the top surface, following the manufacturer's instructions.

Cut the fabric into random widths.

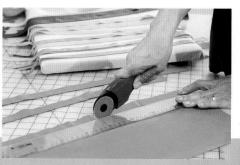

Arrange the strips atop the interfacing, overlapping each by about ⅜" (1cm), and iron.

Turn the fabric over and trace round objects onto the paper. Cut out the circles and remove the paper.

A bunch of different-sized spots are done.

Once the rest of the quilt front is finished, place the spots on the cactus, and iron to affix them.

Layer the quilt front with the appliquéd checkered fabric cactus, the batting, and the backing, and quilt it.

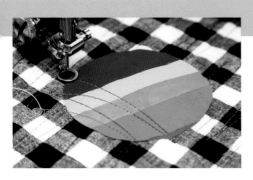

Using No. 30 rainbow thread, sew in a zig-zag free motion over the spots.

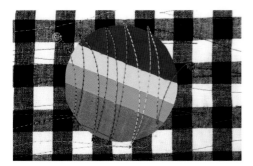

After the decorative stitches have been applied to the spots, the cactus is complete!

## Dreaming Cactus

Made in 2002

67" x 67" (170cm x 170cm)

Hand appliqué, embroidery, machine quilting, cotton, No. 5 embroidery thread, No. 30 rainbow thread

The second in the *Cactus* series. I thought of the name while making the first one, and started this as soon as I finished the first. The colors are gentle, and rather than triangular thorns, I made round thorns for my dreaming cactus.

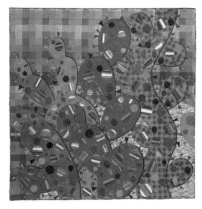

## Cactus in Love

Made in 2002

65¾" x 65¾" (167cm x 167cm)

Hand appliqué, embroidery, machine quilting, cotton, No. 5 embroidery thread, No. 30 rainbow thread

This is the first piece in the *Cactus* series. I was looking at a small cactus in my home when this design popped into my head. Both the title and the design came together easily, and it was fun to make. I finished it in just a month. The second and third in the series also came easily.

**Tropical Seashore**

Made in 1996

78¾" x 64" (200cm x 163cm)

Hand appliqué, piecing, quilting, embroidery, cotton, No. 5 embroidery thread, sashiko thread

When I decided I wanted to make an ocean-themed quilt, a southern island seashore that I hadn't yet seen before floated into my head, and I designed a bunch of images. I think of this as a seashore on some southern island.

## Thinking of Africa

Made in 1987

61¾" x 61¾" (157cm x 157cm)

Hand appliqué, quilting, machine piecing, cotton

I love different fabrics from different countries, and I've collected a lot of them. This quilt is based on mudcloth from Africa. I used bias tape made from printed fabric for the whitish line patterns, and appliquéd them on. My mother made that bias tape for me. Thank you!

## Flower Garden A

Made in 2009

Size inside the frame:
9½" x 9½" (24cm x 24cm)

Machine appliqué, quilting, hand embroidery, cotton, No. 5 embroidery thread

I designed this, wanting to make something "simple, that can be made with free motion." The fabric is just cut and then held in place by sewing around and around with free motion, and inside the flower are tons of french knots! A cute flower garden is done in a snap.

## Flower Garden B

Made in 1997

Size inside the frame:
11¾" x 11¾" (30cm x 30cm)

Machine appliqué, quilting, hand embroidery, cotton, No. 5 embroidery thread

This one has a big, bold flower. Inside are little round cut-up bits of fabric, attached with free motion the same as A, and tons of french knots in the centers.

# Flower Garden Frame

An appliqué where you just sew free motion circles around and around on rough-cut fabric? By adding a few touches, these beautiful flowers will bloom before your very eyes.

**You'll need:**
backing fabric,
fabric for the flowers,
No. 5 embroidery
thread, and some yarn
for the flower stems.

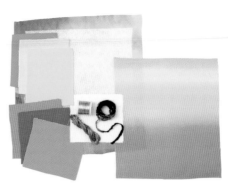

Lay out the composition on the backing fabric, and draw in the frame size with a marking pen that can be erased with water.

First, machine-sew the stem onto the backing with a decorative stitch. Machines without a decorative stitch setting can use a zig-zag stitch.

First, attach the main background of the flower by sewing around and around several times freehand, then place the smaller circles on top and attach them in the same way with freehand stitches.

Add several french knots to the center of the small circles with embroidery thread. Scatter some more french knots around the remaining space on the large circle.

# Alphabet

Here are a red and a blue alphabet, but when I decided to make the red quilt, I thought, even if I use only red fabric, it won't be a pretty red. Adding just a little fabric from the opposite, cool color range into the design helped the red pop out and look much prettier. Alternatively, with the blue quilt, adding some warm accents helped make the blue look nice.

This quilt is mostly blue overall, but just like the red alphabet, there are some warm colors among the blue. I think this helps make the blue color pop. I drew a full-size pattern and pieced it together, then did everything else with hand embroidery.

I really think the alphabet is a versatile thing. When I want to put some words into a piece, Japanese script often doesn't quite fit. But when I try fitting in some alphabet letters… With capital letters, even if the shapes have to be changed a bit to fit into the design, you can still read it, right? That's really cool! There are trad patterns that use letters, but I really have fun doing my alphabets without a paper pattern, making shapes freely and playing it by ear.

**Happy 30th Anniversary!**

Made in 2009

30" x 33½" (76cm x 85cm)

Machine piecing, quilting, hand appliqué, embroidery, cotton

In 2010, my favorite band Jaywalk celebrated the 30th anniversary of its debut. I made this with feelings of, "Thanks for making so many songs I love!" What anniversary should we make as the next goal?

## Blue Alphabet

Made in 2005

69¼" x 62¼" (176cm x 158cm)

Machine piecing, quilting, hand appliqué, cotton

This is my second alphabet quilt. After I made the first, I wanted to make one more, so I decided to make blue the theme of the second alphabet quilt. *Red Alphabet* has a bit of contrasting blue in it. *Blue Alphabet* has some warm colors like orange in it, which makes the blue look more beautiful.

**Red Alphabet**

Made in 2005

52⅜" x 55⅛" (133cm x 140cm)

Machine piecing, quilting, hand appliqué, cotton

At the venue for our biannual circle exhibition, I made this alphabet a little bit every day, and this quilt is the result. I started making it because I wondered if it would be possible to make an alphabet without a pattern. I think an interesting alphabet was made thanks to the lack of pattern. It did have many difficult shapes, though...

# A to Z Pattern

Layout scheme for the blue alphabet

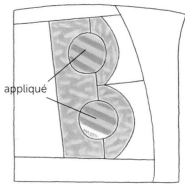

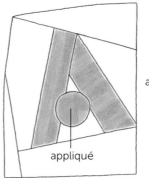

appliqué

appliqué

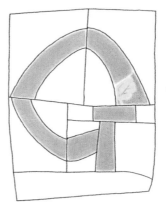

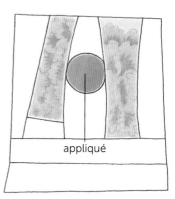

appliqué

## Alphabet Layout Hints

It's perfectly okay to start making a quilt with a general idea of the overall color scheme but without knowing every detail. First, make each block in a color you like. If you do this, you'll begin to see what color you'd like to make the next block. Making one block at a time, deciding the color as you go, is fun and easy, even for large projects. This time, I wanted to use lots of bold, vibrant prints, so there are a lot of strong, assertive fabrics here. Using careful placement of plain fabric is an easy way to make sure they don't clash with one another.

appliqué

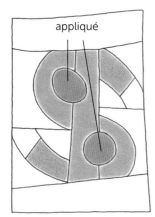

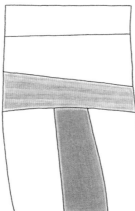

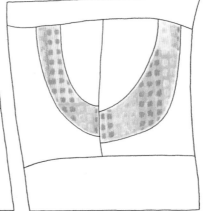

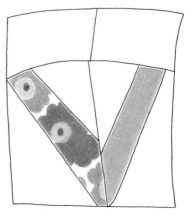

### Thank You Dear JAYWALK

Made in 2004

68½" x 69¼" (174cm x 176cm)

Machine piecing, quilting, hand embroidery, cotton, No. 5 embroidery thread

I wonder how long it has been since I discovered Jaywalk. There was a time I listened to them like I was addicted. They always give me energy and cheer me on. I made this quilt of letters and words that relate to them, to express my gratitude.

Me with the members of Jaywalk after
a show.

## Happy 25th Anniversary!

Made in 2005

54¾" x 72⅞" (139cm x 185cm)

Machine piecing, quilting, hand
appliqué, cotton

I made this for the 25th anniversary of
Jaywalk's debut. Even though I made a
pattern first, the piecing was really hard.
I was so relieved when I was done. I did the
"Congratulations 25th Anniversary!" letters
with a needle-punch method of appliqué.
Can you find the giant "JAYWALK" and
"25" shapes?

Jaywalk's newest album, "STORIES."

When this album came out, I dug up a bunch
of their older stuff and listened to it while
I was working.

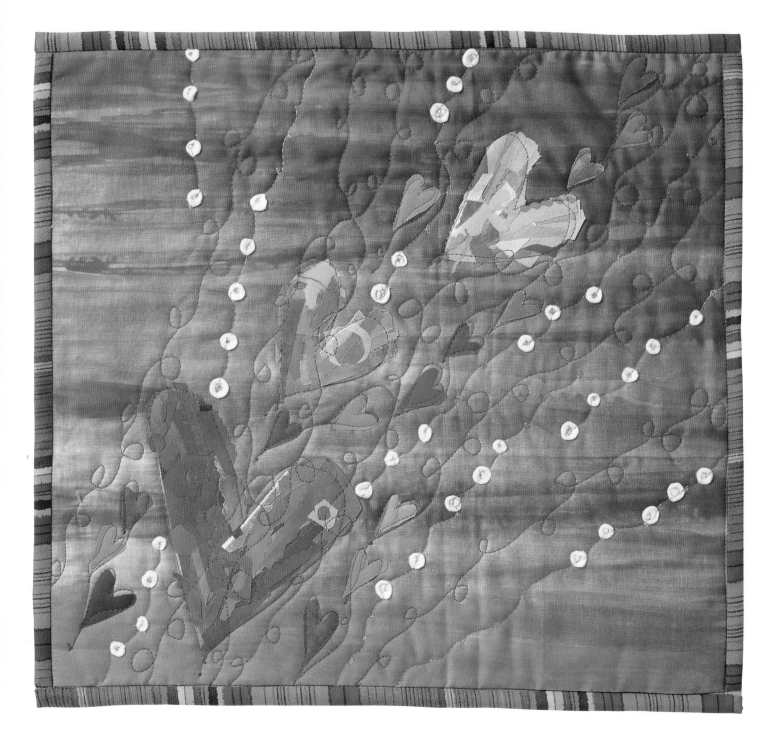

When I used to go to the seaside to collect beach glass, I sometimes found heart-shaped stones along the same beach. Just like the beach glass, these are gifts from the sea, polished by the waves over many years. They're one of my treasures!

For some reason, I love hearts! I love hearts that aren't too cute! I've made many, many heart quilts over the years. There are eight works in my large-sized *Heart* series, but in addition to that there are countless smaller quilts, accessories, and more. I don't know how much longer I will continue to make quilts, but I plan to make at least two more large-sized heart quilts. I hope I can find the energy...

I'm sitting here making the hearts for the quilt shown on the opposite page. I saved the scraps from pieces I made using the fusing method, and I chose from what I had and made hearts. It's really easy and fun—try it!

### Heart IV

Made in 1996

50⅜" x 39¾" (128cm x 101cm)

Machine piecing, hand appliqué, quilting, embroidery, linen, cotton

Most of this fabric is hemp. I made it for a hemp-only quilt exhibition in France. It is mostly made with soft cloth such as kaya, so the horizontal connecting lines stand out in an interesting way.

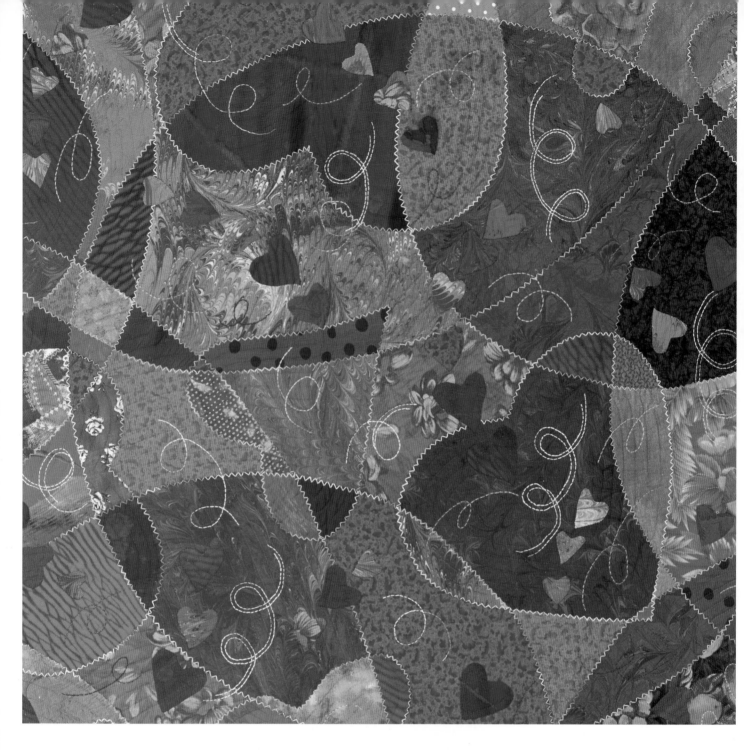

**Heart I**

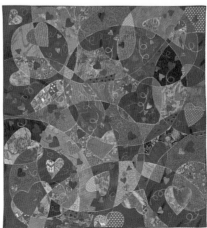

Made in 1992

71" x 68¼" (180cm x 173cm)

Machine piecing, hand piecing, quilting, appliqué, embroidery, cotton

This is the first in the heart series. I drew the design in actual size, freely arranging hearts and circles. Once I started cutting, it was very complicated, and I had a tough time of it, but it slowly took shape, and the process of putting it together was quite fun. Take a look at the piecing method outlined on page 48 and definitely give this one a try.

## Heart II

Made in 1993

59⅞" x 67¾" (152cm x 172cm)

Machine piecing, hand quilting, embroidery, cotton

I do like hearts, but I love log cabins too! So here's my log cabin and heart collaboration quilt. It came to me in a flash, and I made a full-size paper pattern that I cut and moved up and down, so it became this interesting shape.

# Heart I Piecing Method

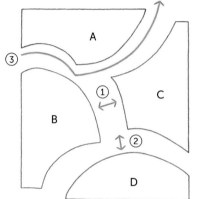

## 1 Choose gentle curves and make a large block.

A

③

① ↔

B

C

② ↕

D

Sew in order from A to D

## 2 Break each block into smaller pieces.

Sew blocks [A] to [C] together to make Block A

Sew from [H] to [K] together to make "c" block

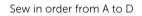

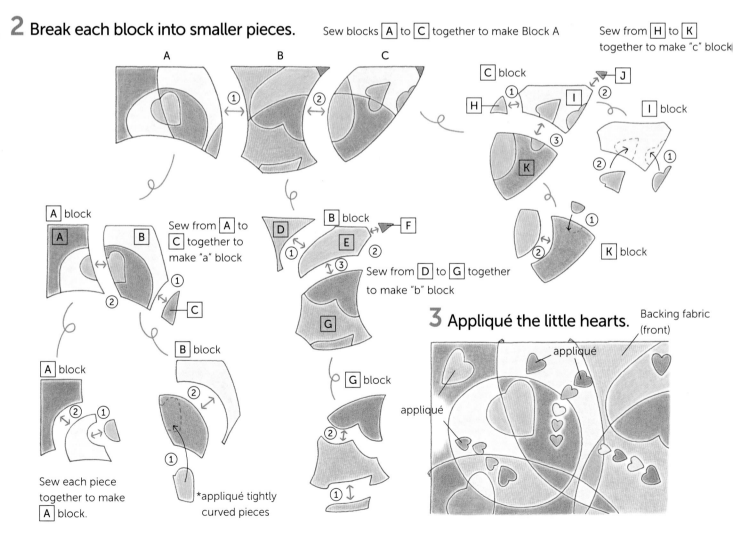

A    B    C

① ↔    ② ↔

[C] block

[H]→ ① ↔    [I]    ② → [J]

↕ ③

[K]    [I] block

② ↗    ① ↖

① ↓

② ↔    [K] block

[A] block

[A]    ↔    [B]

Sew from [A] to [C] together to make "a" block

① ↻

② ↺    [C]

[B] block

① ↻

② ↕

[D]    [B] block    [E]    ② → [F]

↕ ③

[G]

Sew from [D] to [G] together to make "b" block

[A] block

② ↔    ① ↔

Sew each piece together to make [A] block.

[B] block

② ↕

① ↑

*appliqué tightly curved pieces

[G] block

② ↕

① ↕

## 3 Appliqué the little hearts.

Backing fabric (front)

appliqué

appliqué

appliqué

48    All My Thanks and Love to Quilts

# Design Method for Heart II

**1** Draw a heart.

**2** Cut it into four pieces.

**3** Slide the pieces up and down, and add fabric to achieve the completed size.

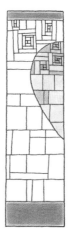

**4** Design the log cabin pattern for each block.

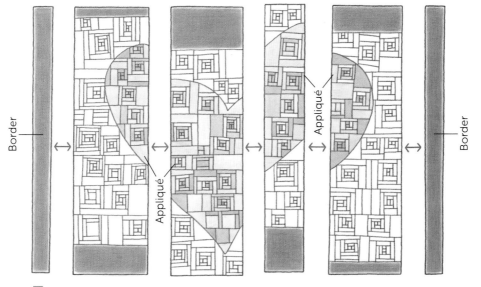

**5** Add a border, and connect each block together.

**Heart III**

Made in 1994

59" x 59" (150cm x 150cm)

Hand appliqué, quilting, embroidery, machine piecing, cotton, No. 5 embroidery thread

With my third quilt in the *Heart* series, I designed something a little different. I had a beautiful triangular piece of murazome-dyed fabric that I highlighted in the piece, putting it boldly in the middle, sprinkling a circle and many hearts around it.

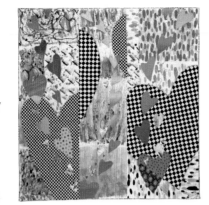

**Heart V**

Made in 1996

61" x 59⁷⁄₈" (155cm x 152cm)

Machine piecing, quilting, hand appliqué, embroidery, cotton

I'd collected a bunch of Debra Lunn's hand-dyed fabric, so I made use of it in this piece. This is a similar idea to *Heart II*. I really agonized over what color of hearts to pair with Debra's fabric on this piece.

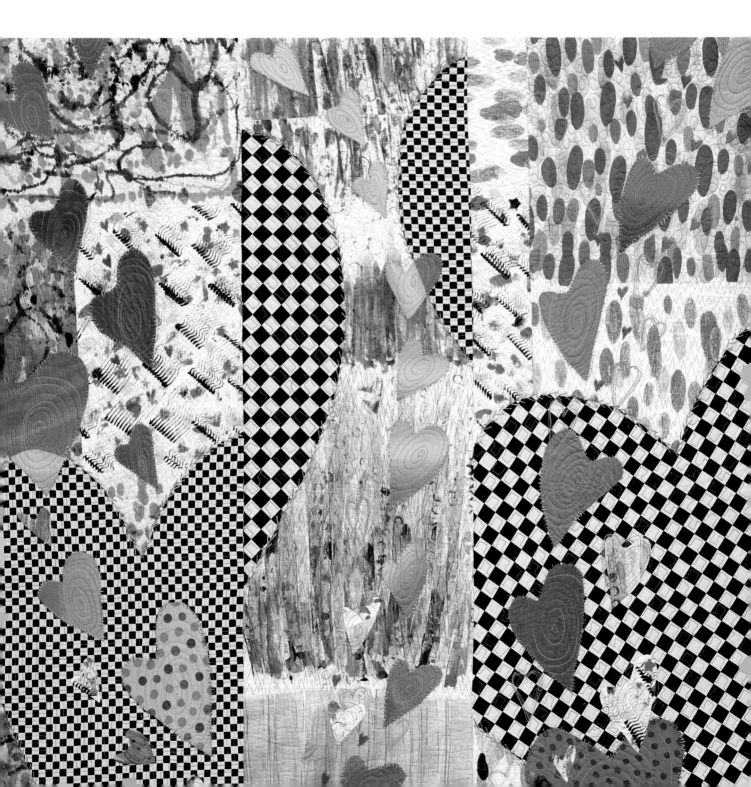

## Heart VI

Made in 2001

67" x 86⅝" (170cm x 220cm)

Machine piecing, quilting, hand appliqué, embroidery, cotton, felt

Up to the time I made this quilt, I'd used mostly warm colors with my hearts, so I decided to make one with different colors, and settled on blue hearts. This work contains Debra Lunn's fabrics. I like the rather mature blue hearts in this one.

## Heart VII

Made in 2002

50⅜" x 81⅞" (128cm x 208cm)

Machine piecing, quilting, hand appliqué, embroidery, cotton, No. 5 and No. 25 embroidery thread

These are the same blue hearts as the ones I used in *Heart VI*, but this time I thought I'd make stripes... I was really able to enjoy the process of making this quilt. I used the fusing method to express lively motion with the circles flying everywhere.

# 5 Circles

### Balloons

Made in 2000
Machine piecing, quilting, cotton

When I decided I wanted to make
something three-dimensional, I settled
on these balloon quilts. I made a bunch
of these beach ball-shaped balloon quilts
with my students. I've gathered together
all the ones we made with the beach ball
pattern. There are balloons inside.

I've always loved marbles. If I find some pretty ones on my travels, I can't help but to buy them. On the left are my newest marbles, with lots of little dots.

I make a lot of different quilt series, and one of them is the circles series. People continue to fight in every corner of the world. As long as there are still humans on this earth, I don't think war will ever go away. But in Japanese "to become round" can mean "to chill out or become mellow," and I think if each person's heart could just get a little more circular…

I was thinking that when I made this, and much before that too, and today as well.

## I Wish We Could All Get 'Circular' I

Made in 1999

180cm x 180cm

Machine piecing, quilting, hand appliqué, embroidery, cotton

When I was making this piece, I didn't think it would become a series, but I've now made six. With this piece, I designed a large circle to fill the space, but it was too large to make without a pattern, so I drew a real-size paper pattern and made it from that.

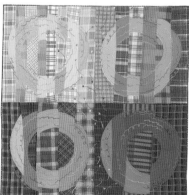

## I Wish We Could All Get 'Circular' II

Made in 2000

67¾" x 68½" ( 172cm x 174cm)

Machine piecing, quilting, hand embroidery, cotton, No. 5 and No. 25 embroidery thread

The second work in the *Circles* series. None of the circles are perfectly round, but I've created four circular shapes using check and plain fabric. I took the four circles made of the colors I love—yellow, blue, pink, and purple—split them up vertically, and slid them around a bit.

## I Wish We Could All Get 'Circular' III

Made in 2001

68" x 70" (173cm x 178cm)

Machine piecing, quilting, couching, hand embroidery, cotton, yarn

In the third piece in the *Circles* series, I used purple and yellow thread, which I love, and made a design on plain fabric. The striped parts aren't straight lines, but lines with curves included, to create a soft, "round" circle.

## I Wish We Could All Get 'Circular' V 'Temari'

Made in 2002

59⅞" x 69¼" (152cm x 176cm)

Machine piecing, quilting, hand embroidery, cotton

I love striped fabric, and I own a lot of it. I thought I'd make my own original striped fabric, so I sewed several different stripes together. I thought they looked a little like traditional Japanese temari balls, so the subtitle of this quilt is *Temari*.

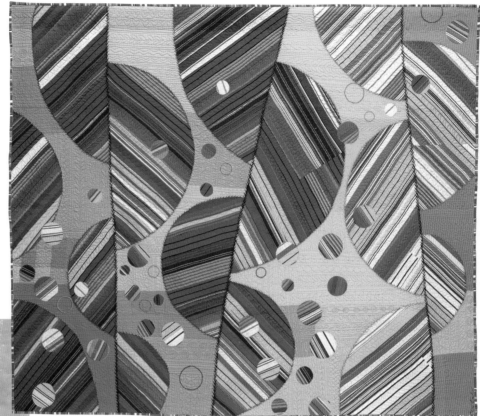

## I Wish We Could All Get 'Circular' IV

Made in 2001

67¾" x 67" (172cm x 170cm)

Machine piecing, quilting, cotton

Here, I've used a three-color murazome-dyed fabric set by Debra Lunn. I wanted to make use of the 8" (20cm) square size, so I kept them at that size and bleached circles inside them. The raggedy circles are so fun!

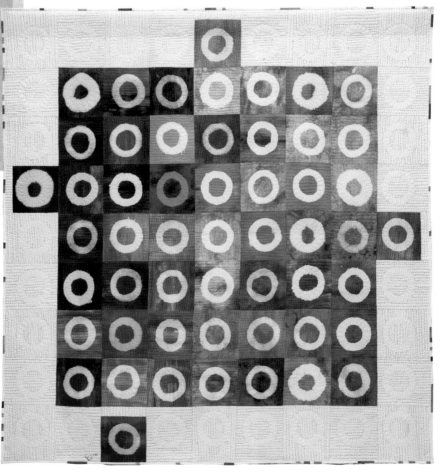

# Making Circles with Stripes

I love striped fabric. I think there must be a lot of people who love striped fabric and have a lot of it. Do you often find that the striped fabric you have doesn't quite match the image of what you're trying to make? When this happens, it can be fun to cut your striped fabric into lengths and sew them together, making your own original striped fabric.

First, gather several pieces of pretty striped fabric.

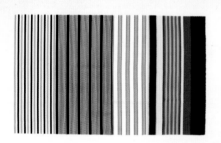

Cut each piece of striped fabric into a random width, and sew the pieces together.

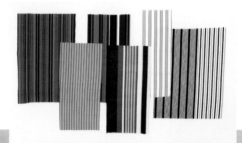

By sewing different kinds of striped cloth together, you can make your own original stripes. Do give it a try!

Cut this into circles, and make a quilt. So much fun can be had with just a simple idea.

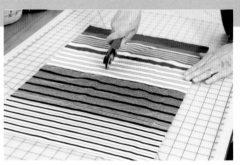

# Bleach Circles

Here are the instructions for making the circles for the quilt on page 60. For my quilt, I didn't thin the bleach with anything, but depending on the fabric you choose to use, straight bleach might be too strong, so I recommend doing a test piece before starting out. I think it would be all right to use watered-down bleach for this. If you don't feel comfortable working freehand, it's okay to draw a pencil guideline.

You'll need some 5" (20cm) squares of fabric, a dish for the bleach, a toothbrush, and some newspaper.

Put a bit of bleach on the toothbrush at a time, and gently scrub the fabric while drawing a circle.

Depending on the fabric, it might not go white immediately, but it will become white after a little time passes.

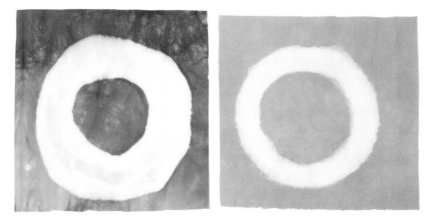

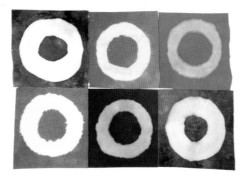

I tried it on a variety of fabrics.

# Log Cabin

I've loved the log cabin pattern since I first began making trad quilts. I stopped using a pattern, and my log cabins just got more and more fun to make. Once the log cabin blocks are prepared and I lay them out, I can see the wide pieces, narrow pieces, pieces going horizontally and vertically, and pieces that are curved. They start to look like strokes of a pencil, and my log cabins develop a sense of movement. They're so fun I just can't give them up!

## Welcome to My Dream

Made in 1992

75½" x 75½" (192cm x 192cm)

Machine piecing, hand quilting, appliqué, cotton

I wanted to try making a piece that combined log cabins and circles, so I designed this. I made the nine central log cabin blocks, then put circles on top, cut out the fabric underneath, and placed the cut-out pieces further out on the work. (Gold Prize winner at the 1991 Quilt Nihon Exhibition.)

## Inclined Log Cabin

Made in 1990

70" x 70" (178cm x 178cm)

Machine piecing, hand quilting, embroidery, Guatemalan fabric, cotton

At first, I wasn't thinking too hard when designing this quilt, but I knew I wanted to use my Guatemalan fabric, so I started making this. Making the log cabin blocks straight up and down would be too ordinary, so I tilted the design 15 degrees to the left, which created a subtle sense of movement. I think it's at an angle where it manages to just maintain a sense of stability. (1992 Quilters Newsletter Quilt Expo First Place winner, 1994 Museum of the American Quilter's Society [MAQS] Contest First Place winner, Fairfield Private Collection.)

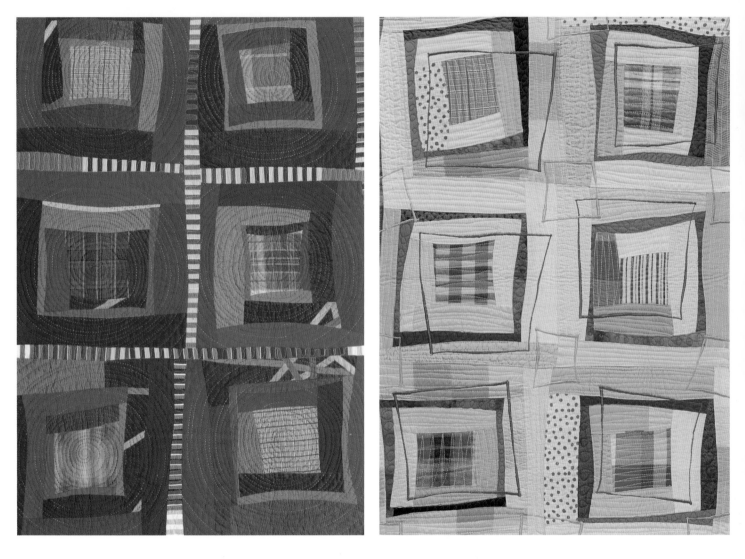

## Log Cabin In Wonderland I

Made in 1997

63¾" x 64" (162cm x 163cm)

Machine piecing, quilting, hand quilting, cotton

I learned this method of using curves to connect pieces for the first time when I took a workshop with Nancy Crow, whose work I love. It was so interesting that I tried it right away. Using curved piecing, I made the first quilt in the *Log Cabin* series.

## Log Cabin In Wonderland II

Made in 1997

60⅝" x 61" (154cm x 155cm)

Machine piecing, quilting, cotton

For the second work in the same series, I thought I'd change the color a bit, and I settled on a blue and yellow color scheme. With this second work, I used the satin stitch on my sewing machine to add some curved squares to create a quilt with an emphasis on movement. (Selected for 1998 Quilt San Diego.)

## Log Cabin In Wonderland III

Made in 1998

64" x 64" (163cm x 163cm)

Machine piecing, quilting, hand quilting, cotton, sashiko thread

This is another log cabin quilt with curved piecing. First I made some little log cabin blocks without a plan. To tie it all together, I split the blue and red blocks, making a large nine-patch-style quilt. I put in a bunch of satin stitch squares too.

## Log Cabin In Wonderland IV

Made in 2007

74¾" x 74¾" (190cm x 190cm)

Machine piecing, quilting, cotton

The plans for my quilts tend to come together as I work. For this one, I started by making several log cabin blocks, then became interested in the white and decided to try making several different shades of white. I sort of feel as though this was when the colors in my works started to change, little by little.

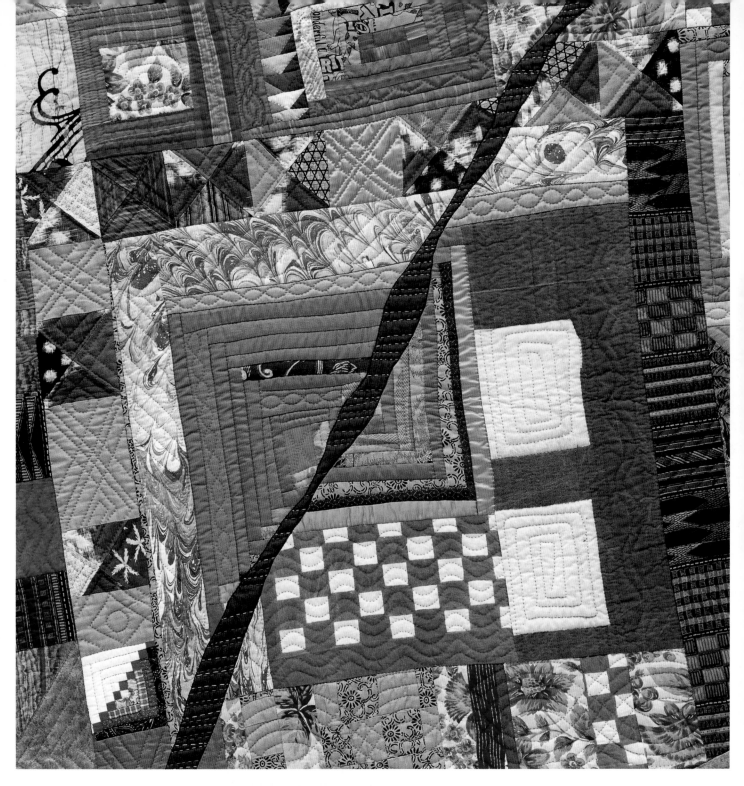

## Broken Log Cabin I

Made in 1990

60¼" x 60¼" (153cm x 153cm)

Machine piecing, hand quilting, appliqué, cotton

I started with the log cabin in the middle, sewing around and around as you do when you make a log cabin. At the end I decided if I just left it like this it would be boring, so after I had cut the whole thing, I appliquéd it onto a background fabric, and my broken log house was completed.

## Broken Log Cabin II

Made in 1991

73¼" x 73¼" (186cm x 186cm)

Machine piecing, hand quilting, appliqué, embroidery, cotton, self-dyed fabric

This whole design came to me when I was looking at some fabric I'd dyed myself. I braced the delicate hand-dyed colors in a border of black and white stripes, and made one of my beloved log cabin quilts.

# How to Make Dandelion Heads

When I first started out, I was making the entire dandelion heads with embroidery, but one day I had a realization. I could probably just put some lace down and embroider on top of it…hmmm. The result: if you put lace down and embroider on top of it, it's much faster! I think any lace would work, so do give it a try.

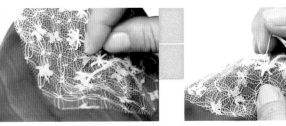

Embroider with six strands of No. 25 embroidery thread.

Decide the position for the dandelion heads and place your lace. One or two layers both work fine.

Embroider as much as you like, then do the stem in embroidery.

**It's Spring**

Made in 1995

81⅞" x 67¼" (208cm x 171cm)

Machine piecing, hand quilting, embroidery, cotton, No. 25 embroidery thread

I made several quilts in a *Spring* series. First, I made a bunch of log cabin blocks without a pattern, then I cut some curved lines, and put borders on two sides, and then since it's spring, I decided to blow some dandelion fluff around. The dandelion heads are made up of lace with embroidery thread sewn on top.

**Double Wedding Ring**

Made in 1991

59⅜" x 59⅜" (151cm x 151cm)

Machine piecing, hand quilting, cotton

I made this for the "New Quilts from Old Favorites" contest held by the Museum of American Quilts Society (MAQS). I thought I'd just use one part of a double wedding ring pattern, and I drew a full-size paper pattern and made it.

## Summer Time in Vermont

Made in 1992

83" x 71¼" (211cm x 181cm)

Machine piecing, hand quilting, cotton

I really do love log cabins. This piece is made of log cabin blocks. The sight of a lake I saw, sparkling in the light, when I was traveling in Vermont was unforgettable to me, so I made it into a quilt. (Selected for the 1991 Quilt National.)

## Warped Log Cabin

Made in 1994

73⅝" x 59" (187cm x 150cm)

Machine piecing, hand quilting, embroidery, cotton, self-dyed fabric, No. 5 embroidery thread, sashiko thread

One day it suddenly occurred to me: No one ever said log cabins had to be straight... So I made my warped log cabin. I made 32 square patterns, each of them warped. At the center of each pattern were little pieces of fabric I'd cut to match the shape of the pattern. I just wrapped thin strips of fabric around these little four-sided figures and they came out pretty much as the pattern dictated, warped squares.

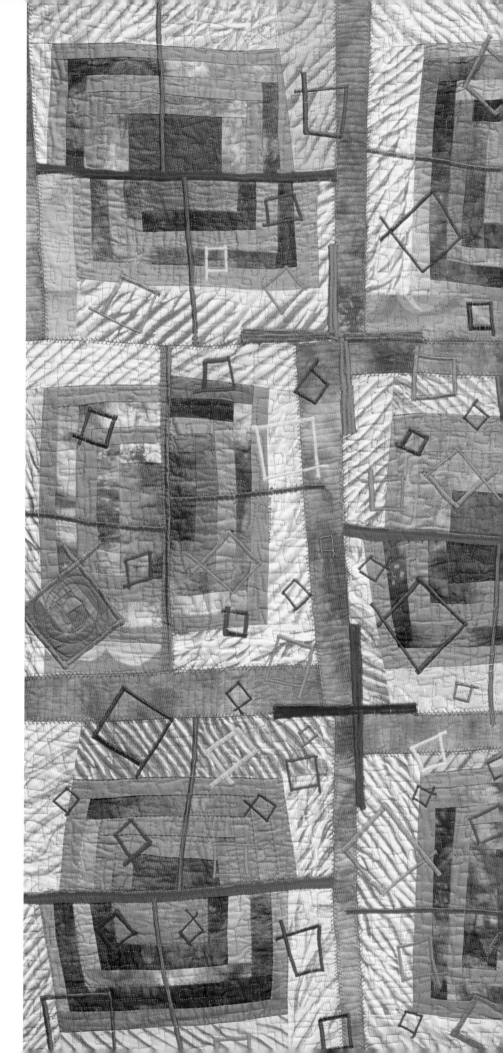

## Half Log Cabin

Made in 1997

58¼" x 55⅞" (148cm x 142cm)

Machine piecing, quilting, satin stitch, cotton, Debra Lunn fabric, self-dyed fabric

I made ten log cabin blocks, stacked them up and cut them in half, then rearranged the halves. The result was a very funny log cabin. I used the satin stitch on my sewing machine to add small and large squares, which was also a fun job to do.

**After the Rain**

Made in 1992

68⅛" x 67¾" (173cm x 172cm)

Machine piecing, hand quilting, embroidery, cotton

I love rainbows! Whenever it stops raining and the sun comes out, I always look for a rainbow. I suggest that everyone looks for a rainbow after the rain lets up. I'm sure you'll be able to find one... For this quilt, I used curved lines to connect my log cabin blocks. Don't you think the white pieces look like water droplets sparkling in the sun after it rains?

# Japanese Cloth

About twenty-five years ago I visited the workshop of Ayano Chiba (she has since passed away, but at that time was a living national treasure). She had fabric in a large wooden trash box at her back garden in the indigo field. She said it was fabric she was planning to throw out. She was really nearly about to burn it.

"Would it be all right if I took it?" I asked.

"Oh, that's fine…" she said.

I snapped it up and washed it right away, and when I was ironing it I thought, "I've got to make this fabric into something," and I think that was the start of my Japanese quilts. The box included some fabric that Ayano had collected, some that she had dyed, and some kimono fabric too. I used it to make *Indigo / Love / Me (Ai / Ai / Ai)*, which is on page 81.

I'll never forget how pleased Ayano's daughter and successor Yoshino and her daughter-in-law Matsue were to see the finished work. Ayano's fabric is also used in *Shooting Stars* on page 80 and in *Once Upon A Time*.

I was so happy to have be able to give new form and new life to the fabric that would have been nothing but ashes in a few days' time.

## Once Upon A Time I

Made in 1987

59" x 60¼" (150cm x 153cm)

Machine piecing, hand quilting, cotton, silk

I collect old fabric. I used some of the cotton and silk I collected to make this, the first quilt in my *Once Upon A Time* series. While I made it, I thought about the people who once wore this fabric.

## I Wish We Could All Get 'Circular' VI

Made in 2003

76¾" x 76¾" (195cm x 195cm)

Machine piecing, quilting, Aizu cotton

I had a lot of Aizu cotton, so I made this entire quile using just that fabric. There are nine circles, but I made each one a quarter circle at a time and then fitted them together, so they aren't exactly circles. I hope that one day all our hearts can get 'circular."

## Circles and Crosses

Made in 1996

84¼" x 84¼" (214cm x 214cm)

Machine piecing, hand quilting, cotton

Among all the traditional patterns, many of them are very modern. I think this is one of them...Some time ago, the first-ever American antique quilt exhibition was held in Japan at the Shiseido Gallery. At that time, I saw this pattern and I couldn't forget it, and finally many years later I completed this!

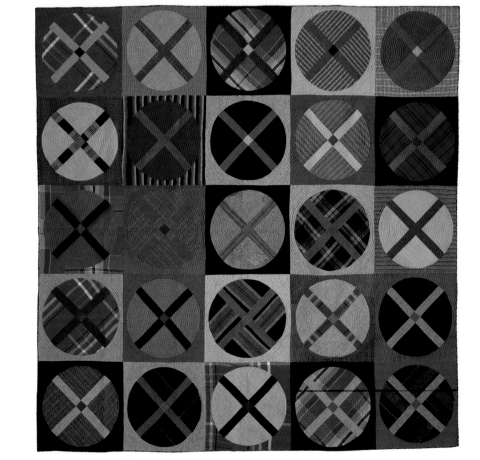

**Shooting Stars**

Made in 1988

68⅛" x 68⅛" (173cm x 173cm)

Machine piecing, hand quilting, appliqué, embroidery, cotton

I used cotton and indigo-dyed fabric that I got from Ayano Chiba, who was a living national treasure, to make this *Shooting Stars*. If you take a picture of stars with a fixed camera, it really does wind up looking like this, and I wanted to try making that into a quilt. I used embroidery to express the dynamic shooting stars.

## Indigo / Love / Me
## (Ai / Ai / Ai)

Made in 1985

83" x 65½" (211cm x 174cm)

Machine piecing, hand quilting, cotton

I wanted to do something with the fabric that living national treasure Ayano Chiba had been ready to throw out, so I made this quilt. There was a lot of damaged, thinning fabric, but I did extra quilting, and it took me three months to complete, a rarity for me. I managed to create a work with a modern image using only Japanese fabric.

# I LOVE THEM
# Quilts

I have a lot of quilts that aren't part of a series. Please have a look! And some things that I wouldn't be able to make my quilts without: my tools.

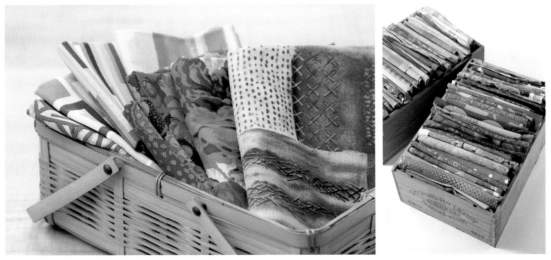

I've got baskets and wine boxes stuffed with fabric... This is plenty, but I've got much, much more, so it's a struggle. I've got so much, I think, "What are you going to do with all of this?"

I almost always use a rotary cutter to cut my fabric, but I love scissors too.

I always want subtly different colors of embroidery thread and quilting thread, so I can't help but have a mountain of it!

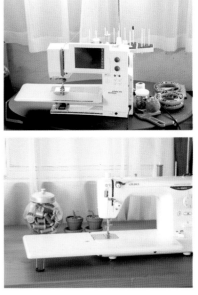

My sewing machines are very important tools. I change machines depending on what I am going to sew.

Made in 1997

61" x 61" (155cm x 155cm)

Machine piecing, quilting, hand embroidery, cotton

**ZIGZAG Lattice**

One day, suddenly the design for *ZIGZAG Lattice* floated into my head, and I whipped up this piece. I say I whipped it up, but it's trickier than it looks. The piecing was OK, but I remember it being very difficult to fit the red squares between what I'd pieced together.

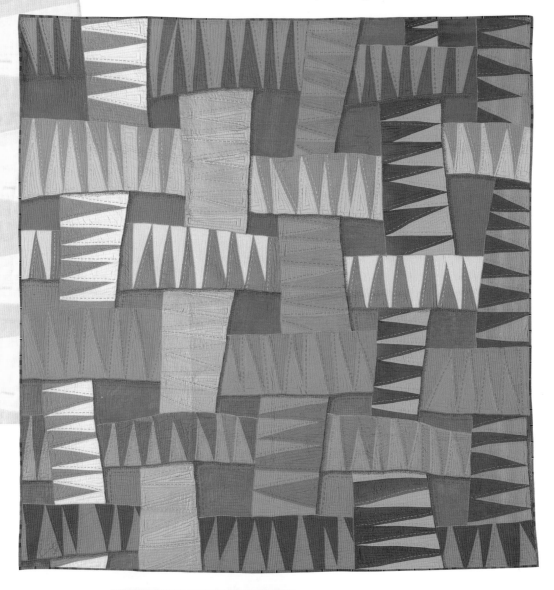

**Stripe I**

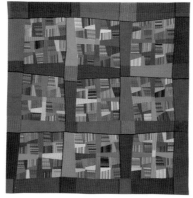

Made in 2006

74" x 74" (188cm x 188cm)

Machine piecing, quilting, hand embroidery, cotton

I received a bunch of samples of Kaffe Fassett's striped fabric, so I designed this quilt with them. I put four of the little pinwheel-shaped blocks together, made nine larger blocks, and tied it all together with blue fabric. It seemed a little flat to me, so I made some shadows with embroidery, which made it a little more three-dimensional and energetic.

Made in 1987

61" x 59" (155cm x 150cm)

Machine piecing, hand appliqué, quilting, embroidery, cotton,
No. 25 embroidery thread

### Polka Dot Fire Brigade

One day, while out collecting data for a book, who should appear
before me but the vocalist from the girl rock band Polka Dot Fire
Brigade! I had been to their concerts many times. Everyone in
the group is full of tremendous power. The illustrations here were
drawn by that vocalist. I remember how much fun I had making this.
I wonder where they all are now?

## TANABATA

Made in 1988

87¾" x 66⅞" (223cm × 170cm)

Machine piecing, hand appliqué, quilting, embroidery, cotton

Sendai, Japan, has long been famous for its Tanabata Festival. I have many happy memories of being taken to the festival when I was a child, but once I grew up I didn't really go anymore. But when I do go sometimes, I am always impressed by the wonder of it all. Sendai's Tanabata decorations are all made of washi paper, so that's probably why the colors are so beautiful. I wanted to make that festival into a quilt, so I made this. Can you see the streamers blowing in the wind?

## Flowers in the Sunset Glow

Made in 1991

70⅞" x 70⅞" (180cm x 180cm)

Machine piecing, hand quilting, appliqué, embroidery, cotton

I love flowers, and I love looking at the sky, and I really love watching the sunset! I got the idea for this when I was watching the sunset and thinking about how pretty it would be if there were flowers blooming there, in the light of the sunset. (Folk Art Museum Permanent Collection.)

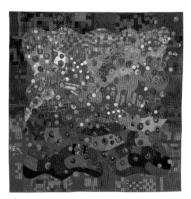

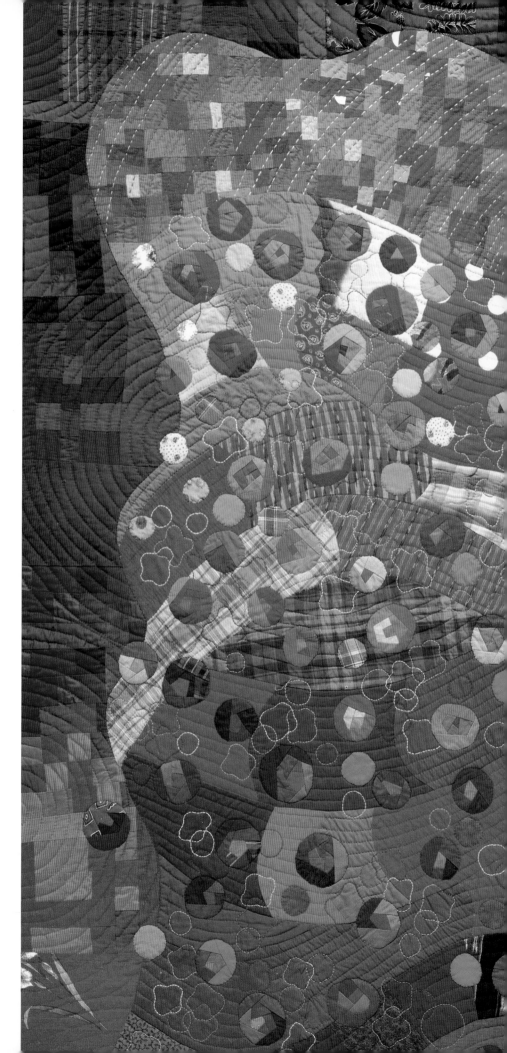

## Empty Sky

Made in 1991

57⅞" x 57⅞" (147cm x 147cm)

Machine piecing, hand quilting, embroidery, cotton, Debra Lunn's fabric, self-dyed fabric

While making this quilt, I just made the design that came to me without thinking about anything in particular, but once it was done, the word "empty sky" came to mind. In Buddhism, this means a space without any obstructions, where all things exist. It means a space, a sky, with nothing... In this way, the words and the space become one.

## Start from the Beginning

Made in 2001

59⅞" x 61⅞" (152cm x 157cm)

Machine piecing, quilting, cotton

I had a lot of fabric that my American friends Melody and Laura had dyed, and I made this piece using only their fabric. Many things happen in a person's life. You might feel down at one time, but one day, you're going to lift up your head and be able to move forward again! Surely "something" will be created, and you can start over. That's the feeling I wanted to express with this work. I used triangles to express this "something" and sent them flying up, up to the sky.

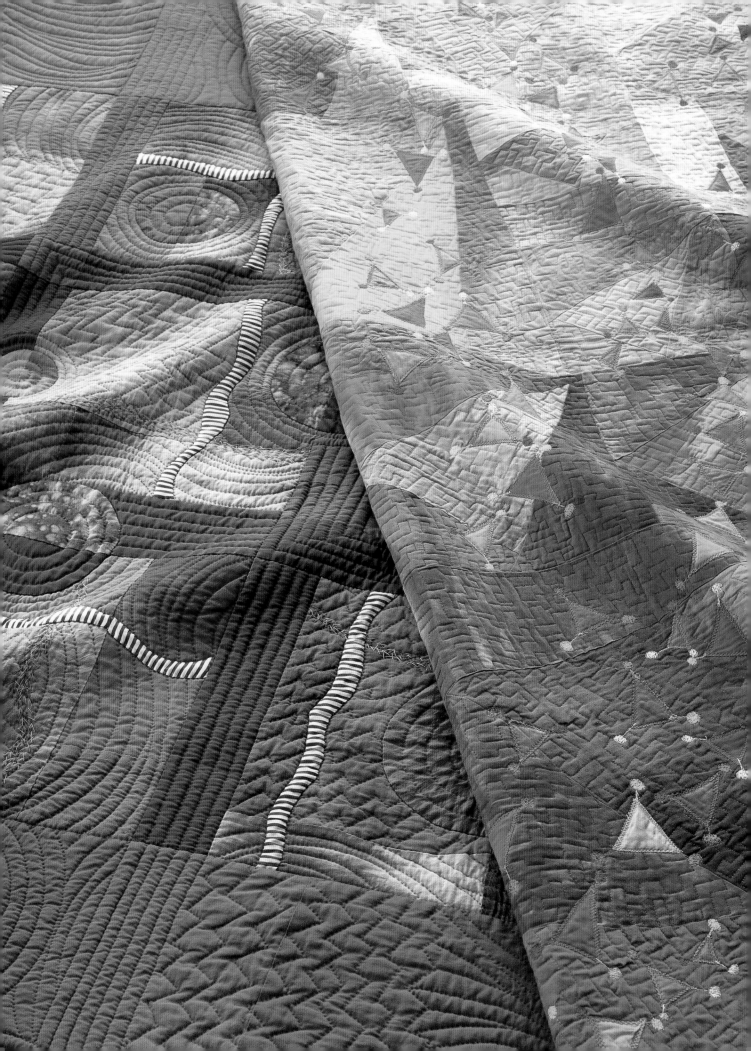

## Have You Ever Seen Flowers in the Ocean? II

Made in 1990

59" x 59" (150cm x 150cm)

Machine piecing, hand piecing, quilting, embroidery, cotton, self-dyed fabric, No. 5 embroidery thread

When I was making *Have You Ever Seen Flowers in the Ocean? I*, I had so much fun that I had to get started on this second quilt right away. The first quilt is made with just the image of the ocean, but this quilt has both the ocean and the earth. I used a life-size paper pattern to make both quilts.

## Have You Ever Seen Flowers in the Ocean? I

Made in 1989

65" x 58¼" (165cm x 148cm)

Machine piecing, hand piecing, quilting, embroidery, cotton, self-dyed fabric, No. 5 embroidery thread

I know of several flowers that bloom in water—I've seen them. But one day I thought, are there any flowers that bloom in the sea? Has anyone ever seen one?

**Happy Rhapsody I**

Made in 1988

68⅛" x 68⅛" (173cm x 173cm)

Machine piecing, hand appliqué, quilting, embroidery, cotton

For this quilt, I made a base pattern broken into four pieces, just like I did to make *Shooting Stars*, and played a happy rhapsody on it with all my might. Can you hear it? The fun rhapsody...

**Happy Rhapsody II**

Made in 1994

60¼" x 60¼" (153cm x 153cm)

Machine piecing, quilting, embroidery, cotton

This is a work I created when I first started making machine quilts. I made log cabins with circles, triangles, and squares, and I appliquéd these onto a backing. When I look at it now, I think my work was a little rough! But then I also remember how much fun I had quilting on my sewing machine.

## Keiko Goke

Born in Sendai, Japan. Graduated from Setsu Mode Seminar and became an illustrator. At that time Goke encountered patchwork, and it has been forty years since she started making things self-taught. She has operated a home classroom for thirty years, and her class exhibitions have totalled nineteen. Goke has entered and won many contests both in Japan and abroad. Her activities have grown to be more and more international, as she has been invited to participate in contemporary quilt exhibitions, held classes, and put on solo shows. Goke is the Chairperson of Quilt Circle Kei and a Nihon Vogue Quilt school instructor.

To learn more, visit:
*http://www.keikogoke.com.*

### Personal History

| | |
|---|---|
| 1970 | Encounters quilts and begins making them, self-taught |
| 1978 | Starts Quilt Circle Kei (home classroom) |
| 1980, 1982 | Group exhibitions in Shibuya and Ikebukuro Tobu Department Stores |
| 1987 | Encounters many contemporary quilts in the United States |
| 1992–2005 | Participates in NHK Oshare Kobo Craft Festivals Nationwide (Tokyo, Sapporo, Sendai, Nagoya, Osaka, Fukuoka, Kashiwa, Kawagoe, etc.) |
| 1997 | Works as an instructor at Nihon Vogue Quilt School |

### Award History

| | |
|---|---|
| 1980 | Sankei Publishing Sunny Day Magazine Contest Grand Prix Winner |
| 1983–1984 | Magazine House "Croissant Magazine"" Golden Needle Exhibition" prizewinner, selected artist. |
| 1984 | Shueisha "Non-no" contest, second place |
| 1989 | Bronze Award in the"Quilt Nihon Exhibition" presented by the Japan Handicraft Instructors' Association |
| 1990 | Won three prizes in "Quilt Expo II," of which one was the Most Innovative New Original Design prize (Denmark) |
| 1991 | America Folk Art Museum Contest prizewinner, "Quilt National '91" prizewinner (United States) Gold Award in the "Quilt Nihon Exhibition" presented by the Japan Handicraft Instructors' Association |
| 1992 | Won two prizes in "Quilt Expo III," one of which was the Best of Show prize (Netherlands) AQS Quilt Show Special Prize |
| 1993 | AQS Quilt Show, third prize (United States) |
| 1994 | MAQS Contest, first prize (United States) |
| 1995 | MAQS Contest prizewinner (United States) |
| 1998 | "Quilt San Diego" prizewinner (United States) |

### Exhibitions

| | |
|---|---|
| 1991–1996 | Invited to Participate in International Quilt Festival "Hands All Around" (United States) |
| 1993 | Participated in Quilt Exhibition held by Leone-Nii Gallery (United States) Participated in Asahi Shimbun exhibition "Quilt 20 People" |
| 1994 | Participated in "Quilt Art Contemporary View" (Germany) |
| 1995 | Participated in "In the Light of Giverny" (France) |
| 1997 | Participated in "Fantastic Fibers" at the Yeiser Art Center (United States) |
| 2002 onward | Participated in International Quilt Festival at Tokyo Dome |
| 2003 | Participated in Asahi Shimbun's "Ten Major Quilt Artists" exhibitions |
| 2009 | Participated in International Quilt Week Osaka, Sapporo, Yokohama, and Kumamoto |

### Solo Shows

| | |
|---|---|
| 1995 | Two Street Studio   (United States) |
| 1997 | Waikato Museum of Art and History   (New Zealand) Living Design Gallery (Living Design Center OZONE) (Tokyo, Japan) |
| 2003 | Exhibitions in Germany (Munich), Denmark (two locations) |
| 2005 | Exhibition at the International Quilt Festival (United States) |
| 2006 | United States (Santa Monica) |

### Seminars Overseas

| | |
|---|---|
| 1992 onward | United States, Taiwan, Australia, New Zealand, Canada, Denmark, Germany, Korea, and more. |

### Publications

| | |
|---|---|
| 1991 | *Iro, Iro, Iro no Patchwork Quilt* Fujinseikatsu-sha |
| 1992 | *Patchwork Quilts* (co-written) NHK Publishing |
| 1994 | *Freestyle Prism Quilts* Fujinseikatsu-sha |
| 1995 | *Shiki no Quilt* Patchwork Tsushin-sha |
| 1996 | *Nihon no Nuno de Tanoshimu Quilt* (co-written) NHK Publishing |
| 1997 | *Iro to Katachi, Ikiiki Asobu Patchwork* NHK Publishing |
| 1999 | *Goke Keiko no Quilt Wonderland* Fujinseikatsu-sha |
| 2005 | Participated in *Kaffe Fassett's Quilt Road*, Rowan Publications |

# How to Make the Quilts

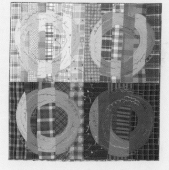

My House   98

Tropical Seashore   100

Red Alphabet   102

Heart VII   104

I Wish We Could all Get 'Circular' II   106

Warped Log Cabin   108

Indigo / Love / Me (Ai / Ai / Ai)   110

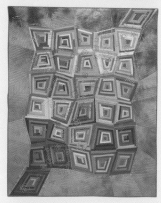

**Things to keep in mind when making the quilts in this book:**

- The numbers on the diagrams represent centimeters.

- With all the diagrams and patterns, as long as there is no designated cutting point, they are all displayed with measurements as a finished piece. When cutting fabric, add a 1 to 2 centimeter seam allowance. If there is a dotted line but no specific instructions, this represents a quilting line.

- The sizes of the finished works represent the size as made according to the diagram. Please be aware the size can change slightly depending on how they are sewn.

# My House FROM PAGE 19

## Materials

**Patchwork fabric:** murazome-dyed fabric and plain scraps.

**Border fabric:** dark blue murazome-dyed fabric 60cm × 200cm, dark purple murazome-dyed fabric 30cm × 30cm.

**Backing fabric:** thin quilting cotton 110cm × 440cm.

**Binding fabric:** violet-blue, murazome-dyed fabric 40cm × 820cm.

**Finished Size:** 198cm × 198cm.

## Order of Assembly

**1.** Make 16 house blocks. They can be made without a paper pattern, so be free with the design and make some interesting houses.

**2.** Make a lattice with strip piecing. It's handy to make a lot of the thin striped fabric used for the lattice when you have the time and set it aside.

**3.** Sew together (1) and (2), and make the central part. When you sew the houses together, adjust the size of the lattice.

**4.** Sew the border on to (3) and the quilt top is done.

**5.** Add a thin layer of batting and the backing fabric to (4), and baste it. Do the quilting with free motion, starting from the center.

**6.** After the quilting is done, tidy up the edges around (5), and do the binding.

## Layout

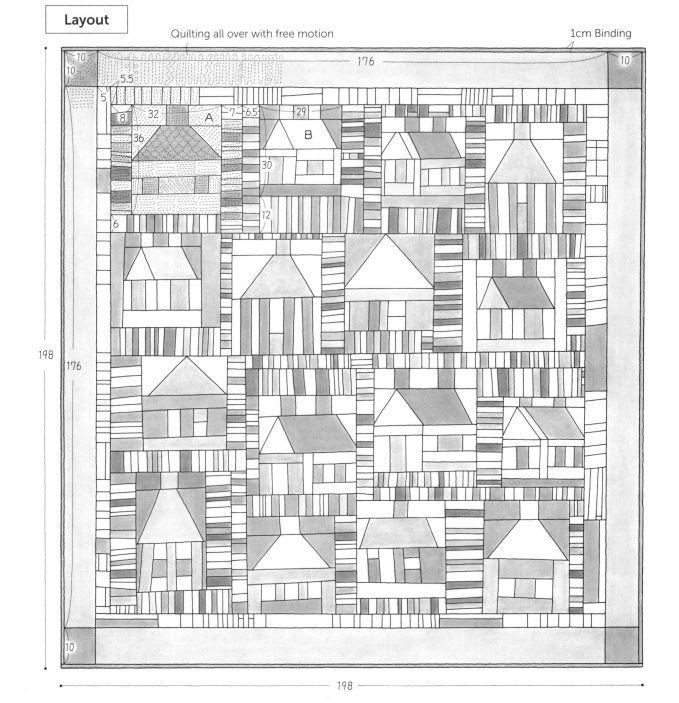

## Piecing

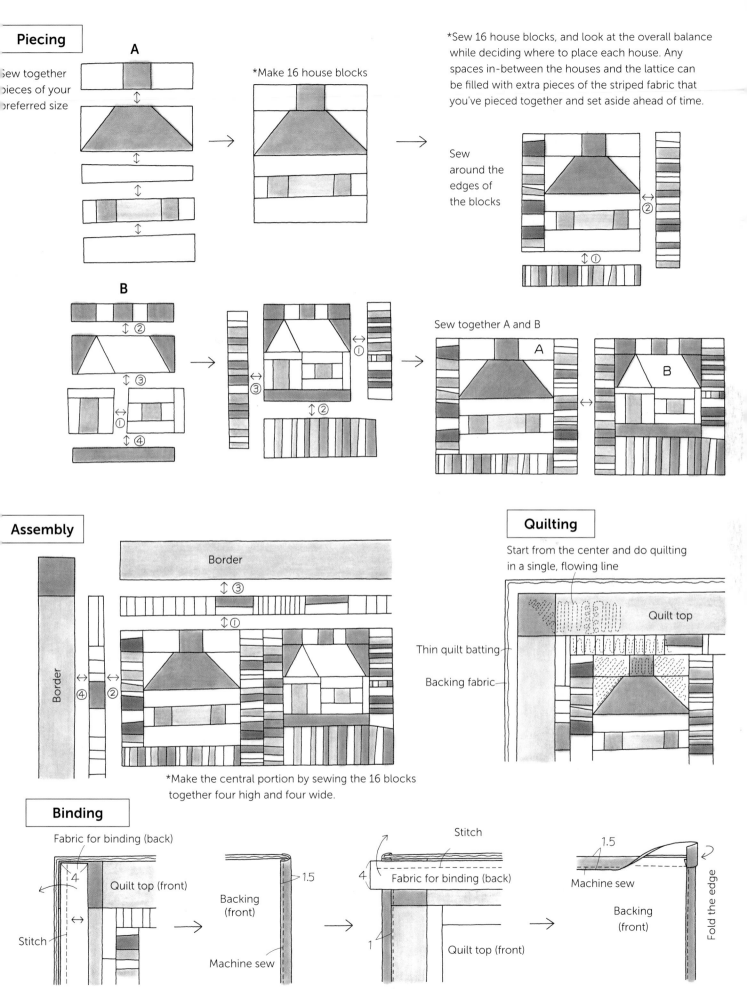

**A**

Sew together pieces of your preferred size

*Make 16 house blocks

*Sew 16 house blocks, and look at the overall balance while deciding where to place each house. Any spaces in-between the houses and the lattice can be filled with extra pieces of the striped fabric that you've pieced together and set aside ahead of time.

Sew around the edges of the blocks

**B**

Sew together A and B

## Assembly

Border

Border

*Make the central portion by sewing the 16 blocks together four high and four wide.

## Quilting

Start from the center and do quilting in a single, flowing line

Quilt top

Thin quilt batting

Backing fabric

## Binding

Fabric for binding (back)

Quilt top (front)

Stitch

Backing (front)

Machine sew

1.5

Stitch

Fabric for binding (back)

Quilt top (front)

1.5

Machine sew

Backing (front)

Fold the edge

# Tropical Seashore FROM PAGE 32

## Materials

Patchwork and appliqué fabric: scrap fabric.

Border fabric: geometric print fabric 40cm × 200cm.

Backing, batting: 110cm × 440cm.

Fabric for binding: green-blue plain fabric 4cm × 740cm, No. 5 embroidery thread, multicolored sashiko thread in various colors.

Finished Size: 200cm × 163cm.

## Order of Assembly

**1.** Make blocks with patchwork and appliqué, using the layout diagram as a guide. Appliqué for blocks A, B, and C are explained on page 101. Make the other appliqué blocks the same way. Make the center area by sewing the blocks together. Around (1), attach the geometric print border fabric and the quilt top is complete.

**2.** Add quilt batting and backing fabric to make three layers, baste, and quilt it. Do the quilting around the border to match the print, and stitch in the ditch around the pieces and appliqué.

**3.** Once the quilting is done, do the embroidery. Stitch freely using colors and designs as you like. Here, I used No. 5 embroidery thread and multicolored sashiko thread.

**4.** Tidy up the edges around (4) and do the binding.

## Layout

Cover the whole thing in stitches

Quilting to match the pattern on the fabric

Appliqué

1cm Binding

*Use any color of embroidery thread, using No. 5 embroidery thread or a single strand of multicolored sashiko thread.

*Stitch in the ditch for all pieces and appliqué.

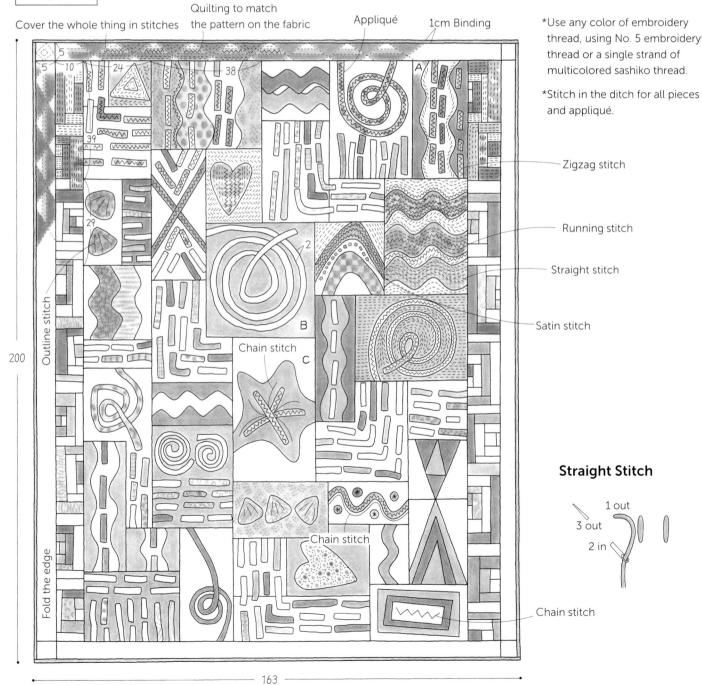

Zigzag stitch

Running stitch

Straight stitch

Satin stitch

Chain stitch

Outline stitch

Fold the edge

Chain stitch

### Straight Stitch

1 out
3 out
2 in

Chain stitch

## Appliqué

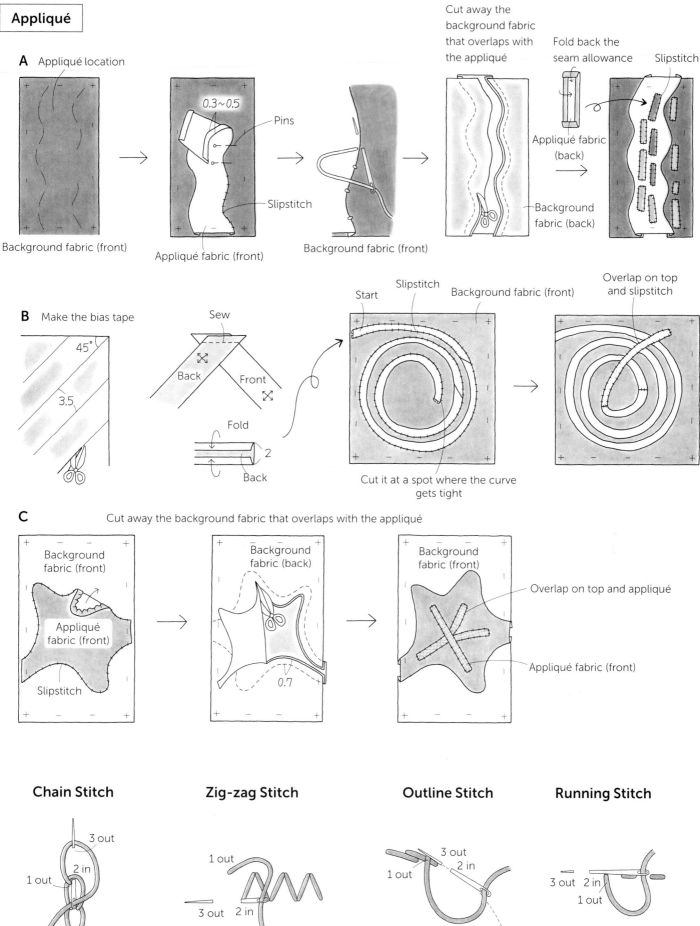

**A**

Appliqué location

0.3~0.5

Pins

Slipstitch

Background fabric (front)

Appliqué fabric (front)

Slipstitch

Background fabric (front)

Cut away the background fabric that overlaps with the appliqué

Fold back the seam allowance

Slipstitch

Appliqué fabric (back)

Background fabric (back)

**B** Make the bias tape

45°

3.5

Sew

Back

Front

Fold

2

Back

Start

Slipstitch

Background fabric (front)

Cut it at a spot where the curve gets tight

Overlap on top and slipstitch

**C** Cut away the background fabric that overlaps with the appliqué

Background fabric (front)

Appliqué fabric (front)

Slipstitch

Background fabric (back)

0.7

Background fabric (front)

Overlap on top and appliqué

Appliqué fabric (front)

### Chain Stitch

3 out

2 in

1 out

### Zig-zag Stitch

1 out

3 out   2 in

### Outline Stitch

3 out
2 in

1 out

### Running Stitch

3 out   2 in
1 out

# Red Alphabet FROM PAGE 39

## Materials

Patchwork and appliqué fabric: scrap fabric.

Border fabric: red and blue print 110cm × 140cm.

Backing and thin quilt batting: 110cm × 300cm each.

Binding fabric: red stripes 4cm × 560cm.

Finished Size: 133cm × 140cm.

## Order of Assembly

**1.** Make alphabet blocks without a pattern. Use the layout diagram as a guide, and make blocks from A to Z with patchwork and appliqué. In order to conform to the measurements, add long thin pieces of fabric, then sew the blocks together. Instructions for A, G, and M are shown on page 103. Make the other blocks in a similar fashion.

**2.** Once the central portion is finished, sew a border around (1), and the quilt top is done.

**3.** Add the batting and quilt backing to (2), and baste. Do free motion quilting around the entire quilt. Do quilting around the border to match the print.

**4.** Once the quilting is done, trim the edges around (3), and sew on the binding, doing vertical edges first, then horizontal.

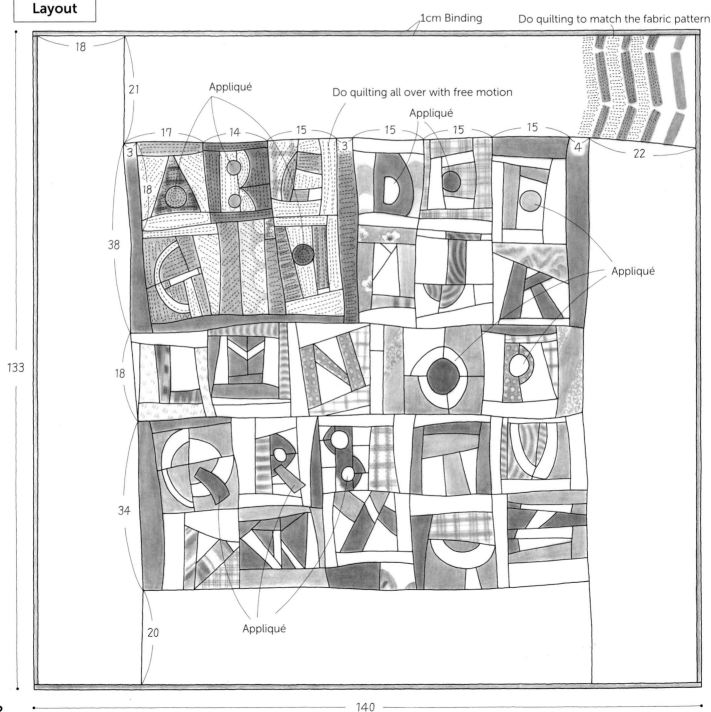

Layout

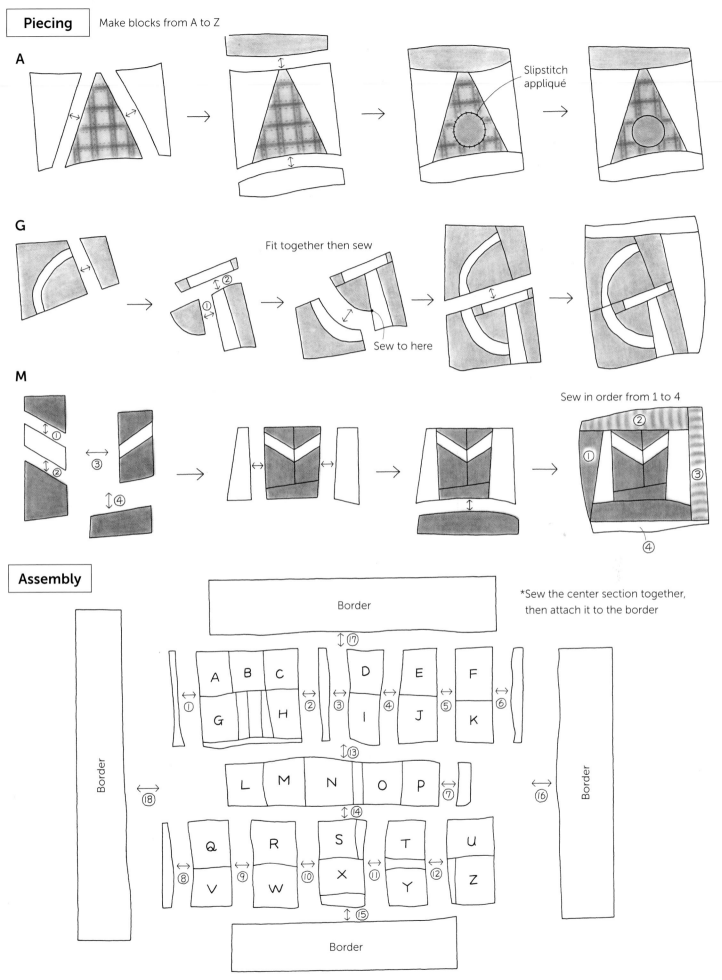

# Piecing

Make blocks from A to Z

**A**

Slipstitch appliqué

**G**

Fit together then sew

Sew to here

**M**

Sew in order from 1 to 4

# Assembly

Border

*Sew the center section together, then attach it to the border

Border

Border

Border

# Heart VII FROM PAGE 54

## Materials

Patchwork and appliqué fabric: scrap fabric.

Backing and thin quilt batting: 110cm × 450cm.

Binding fabric: striped fabric 4cm × 690cm, No. 5 and No. 25 embroidery thread in various colors.

Finished Size: 128cm × 208cm.

## Order of Assembly

**1.** Do strip piecing, making two pieces of fabric: a blue-themed one and a white-themed one.

**2.** Put the heart-shaped paper pattern over (1) and cut, making the appliqué fabric.

**3.** Appliqué (2) onto the background fabric, and make five blocks. The background fabric used to make the heart appliqués can be used in other projects.

**4.** Sew the five blocks from (3) together to make the quilt top.

**5.** Add the batting and quilt backing to (4) and baste. Do free motion quilting over the whole quilt, starting in the center.

**6.** Using the fusing technique (see pages 28–29), make circle appliqué fabric and attach them to (5) with free motion.

**7.** Embroider using a single strand of No. 5 thread or 6 strands of No. 25 thread in whatever color you like.

**8.** Bind around the edges of (7).

---

**Layout**  * Embroidery is done with a single strand of No. 5 or 6 strands of No. 25 in any colors you like.

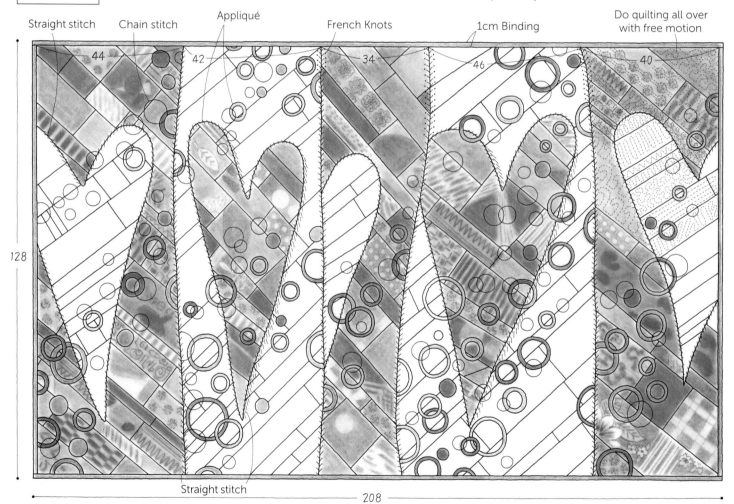

Straight stitch   Chain stitch   Appliqué   French Knots   1cm Binding   Do quilting all over with free motion

44   42   34   46   40

128

Straight stitch

208

## Straight Stitch

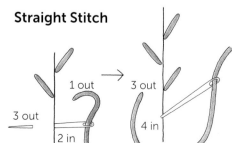

3 out   1 out   3 out   2 in   4 in

## French Knot Stitch

Wind around needle twice   2 in

1 out   1 out

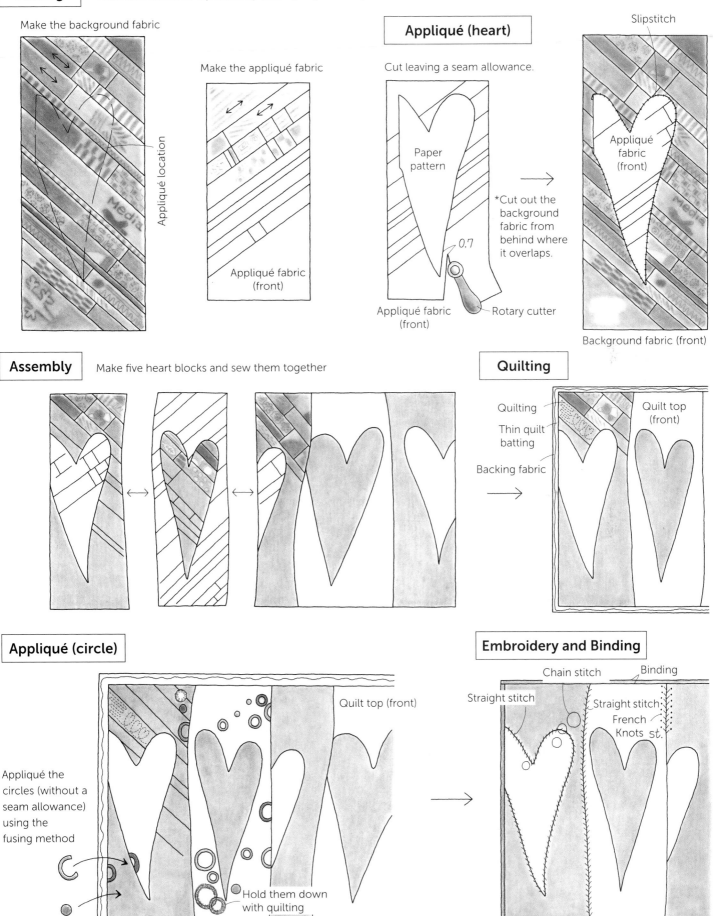

**Piecing**    *Make two colors of top fabric by piecing together strips of various widths.

Make the background fabric

Appliqué location

Make the appliqué fabric

Appliqué fabric (front)

**Appliqué (heart)**

Cut leaving a seam allowance.

Paper pattern

0.7

Appliqué fabric (front)

Rotary cutter

*Cut out the background fabric from behind where it overlaps.

Slipstitch

Appliqué fabric (front)

Background fabric (front)

**Assembly**    Make five heart blocks and sew them together

**Quilting**

Quilting

Thin quilt batting

Backing fabric

Quilt top (front)

**Appliqué (circle)**

Appliqué the circles (without a seam allowance) using the fusing method

Quilt top (front)

Hold them down with quilting

**Embroidery and Binding**

Chain stitch

Binding

Straight stitch

Straight stitch
French Knots st.

All My Thanks and Love to Quilts    **105**

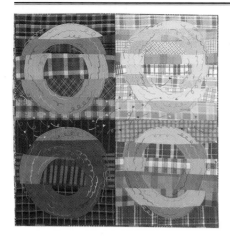

# I Wish We Could All Get 'Circular' II FROM PAGE 58

## Materials

Patchwork fabric: scrap fabric.

Backing, thin quilt batten: 110cm × 400cm.

Binding fabric: check print 4cm × 720cm, No. 5 and No. 25 embroidery thread in various colors.

Finished Size: 172cm × 174cm.

## Order of Assembly

**1.** Make a full-size paper pattern. First, take four square sheets of paper and draw the vertical dividing lines on each. Then, draw circles that are a little bit out of alignment.

**2.** Using the layout diagram for reference, make the four blocks out of patchwork. See details of the A and B blocks on page 107. The other blocks can be made the same way.

**3.** Sew the four blocks from (2) together, and the quilt top is complete.

**4.** Add the batting and quilt backing to (3), and baste. Starting in the center, do free motion quilting over the entire piece.

**5.** Do embroidery with any color you like using one strand of No. 5 or 6 strands of No. 25. See pages 101 and 104 for examples of how to do different stitches.

**6.** After the embroidery is done, cut neatly around the edges of (5) and sew on the binding.

### Layout

Do embroidery with a single strand of No. 5 or 6 strands of no. 25

Do quilting all over with free motion

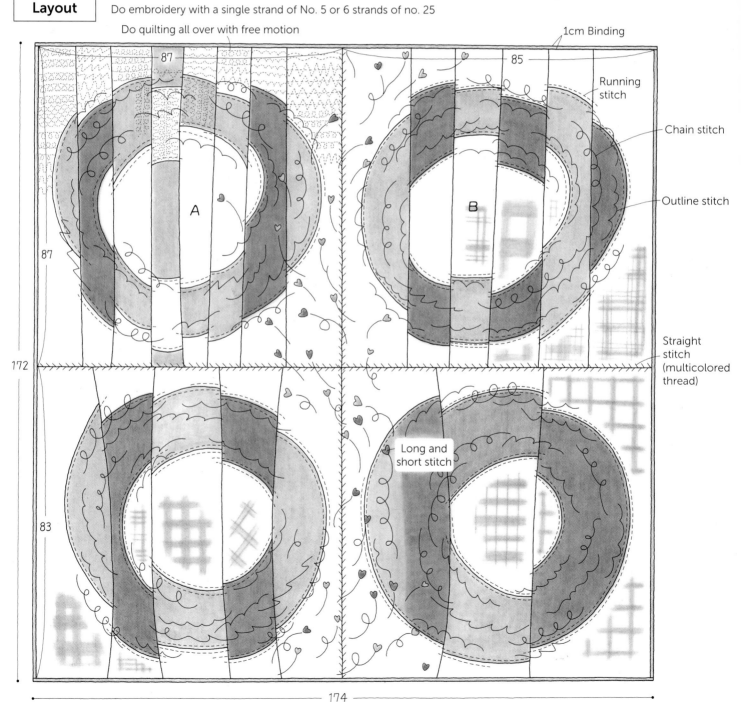

1cm Binding

Running stitch

Chain stitch

Outline stitch

Straight stitch (multicolored thread)

Long and short stitch

87 · 85 · 87 · 172 · 83 · 174

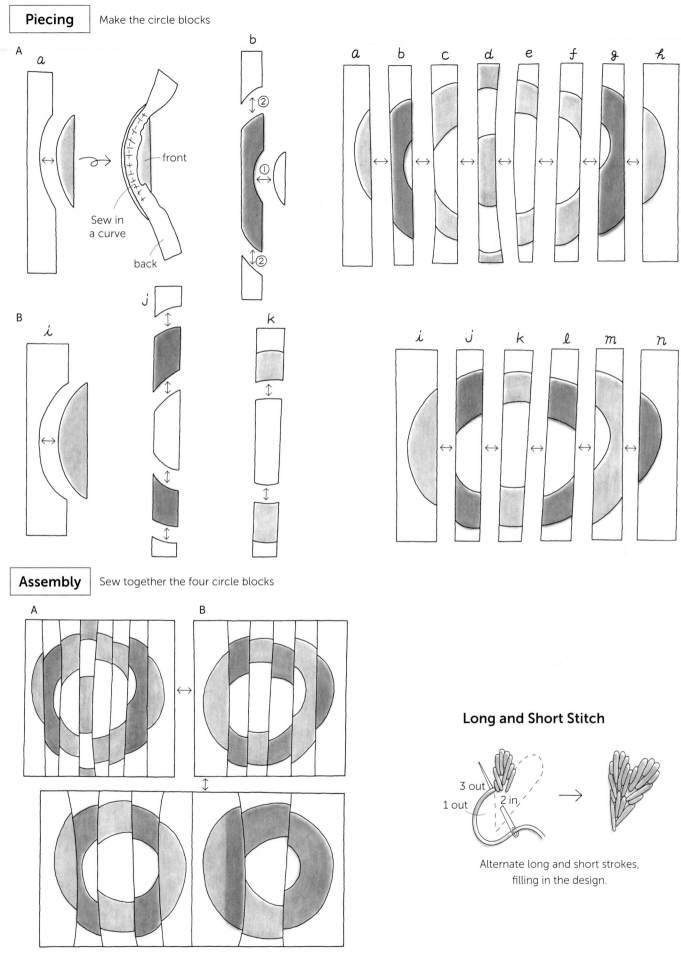

## Piecing | Make the circle blocks

A

a

front

Sew in
a curve

back

b

①

②

②

a  b  c  d  e  f  g  h

B

i  J  k

i  J  k  l  m  n

## Assembly | Sew together the four circle blocks

A

B

## Long and Short Stitch

3 out

1 out

2 in

Alternate long and short strokes,
filling in the design.

# Warped Log Cabin FROM PAGE 73

## Materials

**Patchwork fabric:** murazome-dyed and plain scrap fabric.

**Backing fabric and batting:** 110cm × 420cm.

**Binding fabric:** blue print 4cm × 700cm, No. 5 embroidery thread, and multicolored sashiko thread in various colors.

**Finished Size:** 187cm × 150cm.

## Order of Assembly

**1.** Make 32 full-size paper patterns for each warped log cabin square. The center should be a miniature copy of the overall shape of the block.

**2.** Start sewing thin strips of fabric to the small central square, and go around and around.

The result will be a warped square more or less as planned. See page 109 for help with the piecing method. Make 32 log cabin blocks.

**3.** Patchwork (2) together to make the center of the quilt.

**4.** Sew the border on to (3) and the quilt top is complete.

**5.** Add the batting and quilt backing to (4) and baste. Start quilting in the middle, and stitch in the ditch for each piece.

**6.** Do the embroidery with any color or stitch you like. I use No. 5 embroidery thread and multicolored sashiko thread.

**7.** Do the binding around the edge of (6).

## Layout

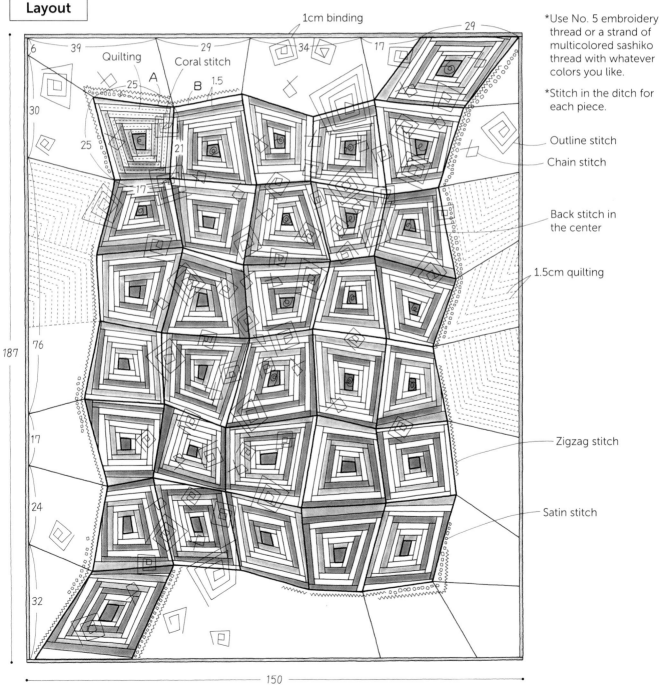

1cm binding

Quilting
Coral stitch

6   39   29   34   17   29

30

A   B   1.5

25

25   21

17

187   76

17

24

32

150

*Use No. 5 embroidery thread or a strand of multicolored sashiko thread with whatever colors you like.

*Stitch in the ditch for each piece.

Outline stitch

Chain stitch

Back stitch in the center

1.5cm quilting

Zigzag stitch

Satin stitch

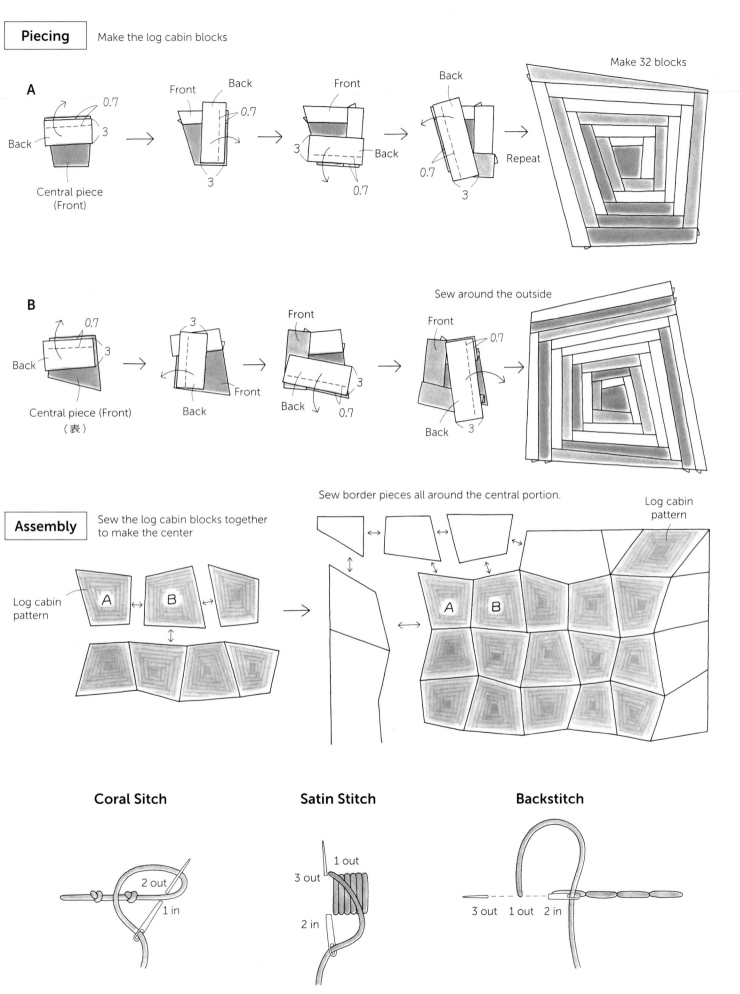

## Piecing
Make the log cabin blocks

**A**

0.7 · 3
Back
Central piece (Front)

Front · Back · 0.7

Front · Back · 3 · 3

Back · 0.7 · 3

Repeat

Make 32 blocks

**B**

0.7 · 3
Back
Central piece (Front)
（表）

3 · Front · Back

Front · Back · 0.7 · 3

Front · 0.7 · Back · 3

Sew around the outside

## Assembly
Sew the log cabin blocks together to make the center

Log cabin pattern

A ↔ B ↔

↕

Sew border pieces all around the central portion.

Log cabin pattern

↔ ↔ ↔

A B

↔

## Coral Sitch

2 out
1 in

## Satin Stitch

1 out
3 out
2 in

## Backstitch

3 out · 1 out · 2 in

# Indigo / Love / Me (Ai / Ai / Ai) FROM PAGE 81

## Materials

Patchwork and appliqué fabric: indigo-dyed Japanese fabric scraps.

Backing fabric and quilt batting: 110cm × 470cm.

Binding fabric: Striped indigo fabric 6cm × 790cm.

Finished Size: 211cm × 174cm.

## Order of Assembly

**1.** Refer to the layout sheet, and assemble the quilt top with patchwork and appliqué. See page 111 for the piecing method to make blocks A to J. The other blocks are made the same way.

**2.** Refer to the method of assembly, sewing blocks together to make larger blocks. Sew the large blocks together, and complete the quilt top.

**3.** Add the batting and quilt backing to (2) and baste. Start quilting from the center, and stitch in the ditch for all the piecing and appliqué. Also, do quilting to match the fabric pattern.

**4.** After the quilting is done, cut the edges of (3) and put the binding on in order of horizontal sides, then vertical, fold it back and do a slip stitch.

## Layout

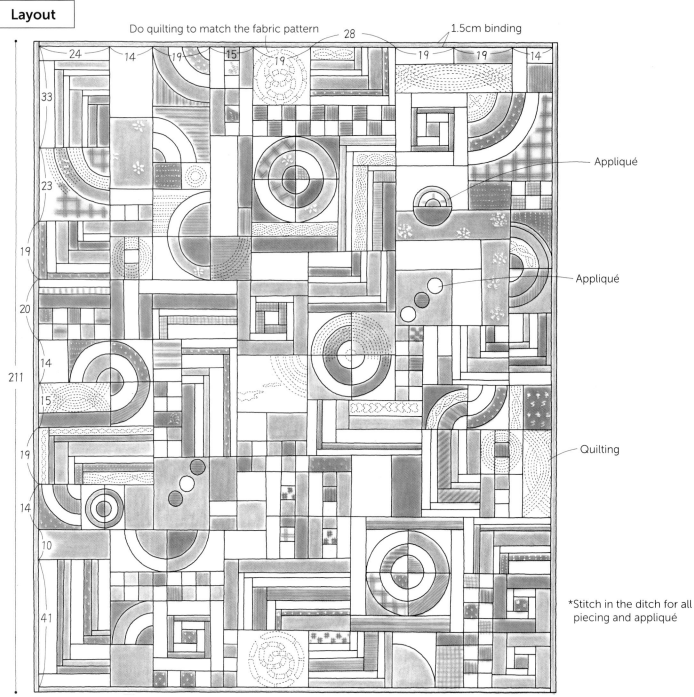

Do quilting to match the fabric pattern

28

1.5cm binding

24　14　19　15　19　19　14

33

23

19

20

211

14

15

19

14

10

41

Appliqué

Appliqué

Quilting

*Stitch in the ditch for all piecing and appliqué

174

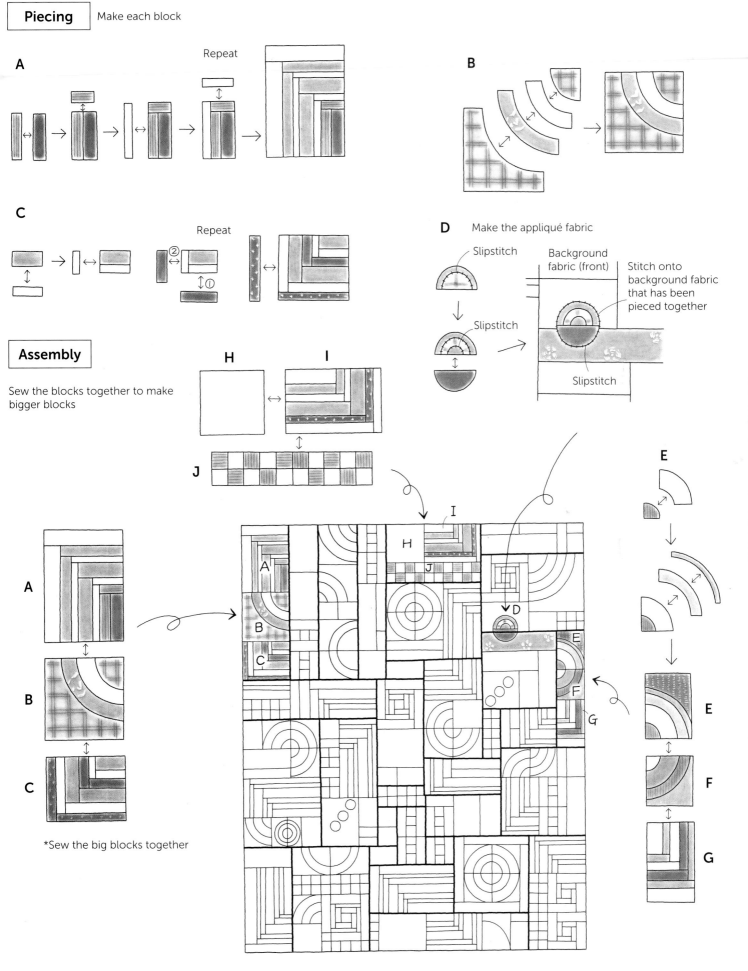

**A**

Repeat

**B**

**C**

Repeat

**D** Make the appliqué fabric

Slipstitch

Slipstitch

Background fabric (front)

Stitch onto background fabric that has been pieced together

Slipstitch

**Assembly**

Sew the blocks together to make bigger blocks

**H** **I**

**J**

**A**

**B**

**C**

*Sew the big blocks together

**E**

**F**

**G**

**E**

**F**

**G**